EYE TO EYE

A memoir of the Nazi Holocaust in Poland

by

Ludwig Charatan
with Carl Capotorto

D1319853

ISBN: 978-0-692-52181-6
Library of Congress: 2015914182

Printed in the United States of America

Author's Note

Most of the events in this book took place seventy years ago and more. I was fourteen years old when they began; I'm ninety years old at the time of this writing. I've waited so long to chronicle my experiences because ... well, I had a business to run, a family to raise, a life to live. And maybe I just didn't want to relive the past in all its graphic detail. Maybe I wasn't ready until now. I've shared many of these stories with other survivors over the years, of course, but not with the definitive sweep and sustained intensity required to produce a memoir. I discovered in the process of preparing this book that the more stories I recounted, the more I remembered — it was like opening a tap. And they keep coming, all with surprising freshness and in vivid detail. Every word recorded here is true. I have invented nothing. My purpose is to ensure that these events are remembered by history, and to bear witness to their terrible unfolding.

Dedicated to Dora Charatan

My wife, my love, my best friend

The Trial, Part 1: Called to Testify

In the fall of 1970, I received a registered letter from the International Criminal Court in Saarbrücken, Germany. I opened it carefully, with a vague sense of foreboding, and as my eyes fell upon the name Fritz Gebauer, the room seemed to tilt and spin around me.

I hadn't spoken his name aloud in decades, didn't know whether he was alive or dead, but I'd thought about this man every day for the past thirty years. Commandant of the Janowska Concentration Camp, monster, madman, a Nazi other Nazis feared, Gebauer murdered my sister, murdered my entire extended family, murdered nearly everyone I knew in my youth. Now, half a lifetime later, he'd been caught and was about to stand trial. The letter was a formal request that I travel to Germany to testify against him.

A husband and father of two boys, a family man living in Brooklyn running a butcher shop — that's who I was now. I'd recently been forced into bankruptcy by a bad investment and was working hard to put our lives back in order. Why did the letter have to come now? I wanted to tear it to bits, toss it into the vat of bone and blood at the back of my shop, and let it dissolve into the offal. But I knew I would not do this. I knew I would testify. I knew that my testimony alone could put Gebauer behind bars for the rest of his life (there was no death penalty in Germany). Most everyone else from Janowska was dead. Who else would bear witness? How would I face my friends one day in Heaven? They would never forgive me. In the end, this is why I knew I would go.

My wife Dora insisted on coming with me. We left

my best employee in charge of the business, asked my mother to take care of our two boys, and set sail aboard the Italian cruise ship Michelangelo on the day before Thanksgiving. (We didn't like to fly in those years.) The German government had made first class arrangements, so Dora and I, survivors who once crawled on our bellies to claw food out of the ground, were treated like VIPs — plush luxury cabin, lavish dinners at the captain's table, fine wine and champagne delivered to our door. (The irony here, I think, speaks for itself.)

We docked in Cannes, took a train to Paris, spent some time with old friends. From there we took a train to Saarbrücken. This last leg of the journey we made in near silence. The behemoth that had slumbered in the background of our lives for decades was rousing now, rising to its feet, lumbering toward us. We could feel its foul breath starting to warm our necks.

As Dora and I stepped out of the train station at Saarbrücken and climbed into a taxi, I could sense her growing nervousness. I said nothing, just rested my hand on hers. We arrived at the hotel, checked into our room, and went down to the lobby to look around. There, we met people from all over the world — Australia, Israel, Poland, England, everywhere — who had traveled here to testify against Gebauer. They would all appear in court the next day, but my appearance was scheduled for the day after that. And I would appear alone. Why? I didn't know.

Now I was the nervous one.

On the morning of my appearance, Dora and I ate breakfast in silence and in silence rode a taxi to the courthouse. What was there to say at this point? We climbed a great set of marble steps and made our way into a large municipal hall. The room was packed and

Fritz Gebauer, Commandant of the
Janowska Concentration Camp

buzzing, spectators jammed in on all sides to watch —
reporters, students, average citizens. We took our seats
a few rows behind a large podium at which was seated
a formal tribunal of maybe ten judges. My breath went
shallow in my chest.

Moments later, Fritz Gebauer, flanked by his
lawyers, entered the courtroom and sat down nearby.
He was unshackled, at ease, didn't appear nervous or
scared. In fact, he had no affect whatsoever. He looked
more like a man waiting at a bus stop on some ordinary
morning than a war criminal facing trial for the torture
and murder of thousands of innocent men, women,
and children. He glanced in my direction, didn't seem
to recognize me. I don't know who or what I looked
like to him at that moment, but seeing him so close to
me brought on an odd, awful sensation, an electrical
charge in my spine, a sharp stabbing sensation in my
eyes and temple. I considered crossing the courtroom
to kill him then and there. This had been a solemn oath
among people at the camp.

"Kill him if you ever get the chance."

Was this my chance?

It would be a piece of cake. He was nearly within arm's reach and there wasn't much police presence. I had no weapon; my hands would do just fine. I looked down at them. Then I glanced over at Dora, thought of our boys. If I killed Gebauer they might never see me again. It would destroy our lives. And yet . . .

The head judge banged his gavel and the room went quiet.

One of the other judges called my name, instructed me to identify myself, and asked which language I wished to testify in. I chose English. They asked me to approach.

As I stepped toward them, an officer of the court walked over to a set of curtains, parted them, and, with the aid of a few others, wheeled out a large raised platform about the size of two ping-pong tables, covered with a heavy cloth. The men peeled the cloth away to reveal a scale model of the Janowska Concentration Camp.

I was not prepared for this.

I knew it would be difficult to see Gebauer again and speak of his atrocities aloud after all these years. But seeing this model was . . . like being back there. A hot sweat gripped my scalp. Why were they showing this to me? What did they want?

As I willed myself to take a closer look, I noticed that some things were out of place: the kitchen was on the wrong side of the street, a bunker was misidentified. The errors were subtle, almost as if they had been made deliberately. That's when I realized: The model was a test. I asked if I could view it from another angle and the judges agreed. I circled around the table until

I found myself looking through the front gates of Janowska Concentration Camp.

In a voice that seemed to come from someone on the other side of the room, or from another place and time altogether, I continued to identify the mistakes in the model. The judges watched and listened closely.

"Der Mann weist was er spricht," one of them said.

"The man knows what he speaks about."

With that, I took my place at the witness table and told them everything:

How I saw Fritz Gebauer stomp on a prisoner's throat to make him choke, remove his boot to let him breathe, then stomp again, over and over, until the prisoner was dead.

How I saw him march naked prisoners outside in the deep of winter, force them into barrels of freezing water, hose them down with more cold water, and torture them this way for hours before finally shooting them dead.

And how on the morning of March 30, 1943, he ordered the murders of the entire nightshift of Schwarz & Company, all one thousand two hundred fifty of them.

Several times the judges looked over at each other incredulously.

"Can you believe this?" their expressions seemed to say.

Throughout it all, Gebauer sat calmly, nonchalant. At one point we happened to glance at each other at the same moment . . . and came eye to eye across the room. I looked at him hard, tried to peer into his soul. Who was this man? He had a pleasant face, reasonably handsome, a bland expression. How could an ordinary exterior like this house such monstrous evil? I could find no answer.

As I wrapped up my testimony, the courtroom broke into chaos. Spectators screamed and shouted at the judges, demanded blood.

"Hang him!" they yelled. "Hang the murderer!"

Now I understood why I had been scheduled to appear alone:

I was one of the only survivors who could testify directly to some of Gebauer's most heinous crimes, the Schwarz factory murders chief among them.

The judges yelled for order but it was useless. Nothing would silence the crowd. Finally, a recess was called.

As the room emptied out, I wandered back over to the model and gazed down into it. It seemed almost to come alive. I thought I saw something move within, thought I heard an anguished cry. I stepped closer, leaned down further, felt as if I could tumble into this miniaturized hellscape and be lost there forever.

Then I felt Dora's hand on my shoulder, her voice soft in my ear.

"Come," she said. "Lunch."

Chapter One

~~~

I was a spoiled kid. Spoiled rotten. As the baby of the family — born in 1925, when my brother Jozek was four and my sister Clara two — my every whim was indulged. And my whims were endless. I was extremely picky about my diet, rejected most of the food put in front of me, insisted on eating and drinking exclusively from my own special plate and cup, never accepted food from a communal dish or bowl . . . and on and on; such a hard time over nothing. I complained my way through most holidays, especially Yom Kippur when we ate two dinners in one day and then fasted for a day. No water, even. And we had to spend hours at temple. I hated the whole thing. I remember being much less fussy about food at the end of the fast, when I would stuff my belly so full that I'd have to lie down on the floor for a while afterward. My father always invited a poor person or two to join our table, in accordance with tradition. That was my least favorite part. I didn't like eating with strangers.

Shopping for clothes was the worst. I rejected every available option until my parents were finally forced to buy fabric and send me to a tailor to have my clothes custom made. What a brat! My brother and sister couldn't believe that I was able to get away with this behavior and chastised my parents for allowing it. But I loved my family ferociously and always found ways to show it. Maybe that's why they tolerated my antics.

I was particularly close to my big sister, Clara, especially as I entered my teenage years. Smart and pretty, a bit of a dreamer, Clara had recently turned sixteen and my parents were eager to see her married. Girls got hitched young back then, and to remain single after your "sell by" date was considered a crisis, especially if you weren't from a wealthy or prominent family. Mother had been building a traditional trousseau and dowry for her only daughter since the day she was born — fine linen and china, good furniture, cash — but my popular teenage sister was still waiting for Mr. Right. There were matchmakers around but city girls like Clara had more modern ideas. She was looking for love.

Clara Charatan

Clara was always in a social whirl and often brought girlfriends home to chat and catch up on the latest gossip. I remember eavesdropping on their private sessions — who was dating who, who was going steady, who had broken up, and so on. They'd squeal when they caught me listening outside the door, and tease and tickle me till I collapsed. Clara sometimes let me tag along with them out in the street — it was a mark of distinction to be out and about with teenage girls. If Jozek saw me hanging out with them, he'd goad me about being the only boy in the pack ... so I'd tag along with him and his friends for a while instead. They were even older, practically adults. I felt like a big shot walking around the neighborhood with the "fellas."

We were still a family of five in 1939, the year everything changed — my mother Helen, father Leopold, Jozek, Clara and I living in a spacious apartment on the eastern edge of Lvov, Poland, about a hundred forty kilometers west of the Russian border. Lvov was a great metropolis in those days. I loved the vibrant bustle of midtown, streets and grand plazas overflowing with shops and markets during the day; nightclubs and movie theaters at night. Many popular songs were written about our hometown . . . and we knew them all by heart. Our apartment was often filled

The house where I was born and raised until age 10 or so, on the eastern outskirts of Lvov

with people, especially on evenings and weekends. My mother and her lady friends would work up a sweat in the kitchen, while my father and the other men played cards or dominoes, usually arguing about the game in progress.

The horror that would soon consume our lives flowed from the simple fact that we were Jewish, but most of the folks we knew weren't very observant. For Jews like us, synagogue was more a social event than anything else. The liveliest part of any Saturday service was the little nosh afterward, when people gathered over schnapps and herring to swap news and gossip or, occasionally, argue about how to interpret this or that passage in the Talmud. I don't remember politics ever being discussed. My father avoided scholarly debate at all costs. He hadn't attended yeshiva and was therefore ill equipped to participate. His business, as mine would become, was meat. Where meat was concerned, he was an expert.

He and mother bought and sold live cattle, and also ran a kosher butcher shop in town. It was closed on Saturdays, like all kosher food places, but religious observance was so loose in Lvov that most Jewish businesses remained open on the Sabbath. Clara always said that Saturday was the busiest day at my Uncle Saul's galanterie in the heart of town, where she worked selling yarns and notions.

What else to say of those early days? Sunday was soccer day, and people streamed in from all over to watch our popular town league beat the competition. I was obsessed with the game, a total natural on the field, and hoped one day to play with the big boys. My brother took girls out dancing on Saturday night. Life was pretty normal.

There was some political friction — many Ukrainians claimed that this part of Poland was still rightfully theirs and that Poland had "robbed it" from them in WW1 — but the only real unrest I remember came from the "academiki," Christian academics, university kids who'd sometimes go on anti-Semitic rampages and attack Jews violently in the street. This was something new, quite shocking, and was roundly condemned by other Christians. Jews and Gentiles got along pretty well, but Lvov had seen its share of pogroms earlier in the century and still had a lingering tradition of anti-Semitic laws and policies. Saint Antone's, the public school I attended, was so far from our house that I had to travel nearly to midtown to get there. I pressed my parents nonstop to transfer me to Zimorowicza, much closer to home, where all my friends went. Why did I have to take the trolley everyday when there was a better school within walking distance? After a few years of this, my mother sat me down for a serious talk.

"You can't go to Zimorowicza," she said. "It's a public school, yes. But not for Jewish kids."

What?

Young as I was, maybe nine years old at the time, these words hit me like a hammer. The very thought was foreign to me, totally bizarre. I knew that Christians went to church and Jews to synagogue . . . but that was about all. I had never experienced discrimination directly and didn't remember my parents complaining of it, either. The Express Wieczorny, a popular evening newspaper, was delivered to our door every night and my mother read it cover to cover, but she never talked politics as far as I can recall. Most of our neighbors, Polish and Ukrainian Catholics, had always been friendly and respectful. And there were plenty of Christians among the boys I played soccer with. We didn't know any difference. The game was all. You played hard and fought for the team . . . period. Who cared which service your family dragged you to on Saturday or Sunday morning? It concerned us only when it threatened to interfere with our game.

I had started attending Hebrew school at age five, like all Jewish boys, and the extra classroom hours often conflicted with my soccer schedule. If there was an important game or practice coming up, I'd whisper to my mother that I was planning to skip Hebrew school, and she'd help cover for me. I was jealous of the Catholic kids — they didn't have to go through this. That was about as much thought as I gave it.

The whole "no Jewish kids" thing simply confounded me. I asked a Christian friend of mine, a student at Zimorowicza, to talk to his teacher about it. My friend promptly reported that his teacher had screamed at him and told him never to ask such dumb questions. I started to pay more attention at school after that, started to watch for signs . . . and little by little, began to notice the anti-Semitism of my Polish teachers. Some were openly hostile toward Jews and made sure to let their students know it. I found the whole thing stupid and pointless — and very disappointing.

As I got a little older, my parents would sometimes gather my siblings and me together to tell about their experiences during World War I. We listened with open mouths to tales of chaos and brutality against Jews. We learned that my grandparents on both sides had lost everything during the war — their money "turned to toilet tissue," my mother said — and that my maternal grandmother and an aunt died of cholera. We were duly awed and troubled by these stories, but they belonged to a distant past. These were modern times. I couldn't imagine that we'd ever live through anything like that.

The fact is that Jewish life was rich and varied

and flourished everywhere in Lvov during my youth. There were Jewish schools and other institutions, Jewish newspapers and periodicals, and at least fifty functioning synagogues sprinkled around the city. By the end of the 1930s, the Jewish population in Lvov had swelled to over 140,000, more than a third of the population overall. There was safety in numbers, and a firm sense of belonging. Lvov was home, and that was that.

It all changed in a flash.

Chapter Two

~~~

Hitler's invasion of Poland began on September 1, 1939. In what would come to be known as the September Campaign, Nazi forces stormed the country from the north, south, and west. We were on the other side of the country, in the east, a good distance away, but it was terrifying nonetheless.

A couple of weeks later, on September 17, 1939, the Russian army rode into Lvov from the east and occupied our city to hold it against further Nazi aggression.

Suddenly we were living under Communist rule. Most synagogues were shut down.

Local businesses were forced to sell off their stock and shutter their doors, including our butcher shop. There was no work for anyone. We subsisted on meager Communist rations, standing for hours on long rowdy lines in order to get staple items like milk and bread, and even longer ones for shoes, clothing, and other necessities. Jozek and Clara managed to find jobs working in government-run shops in town, and my parents, like everyone else, were able to do a little black market business. I wanted badly to get out and hustle, but at only fourteen I was required by law to stay in school. The Russians immediately took charge of the educational system, of course, so I now found myself in a highly militarized environment, strict and rigid, rife with Communist jargon and rhetoric — all in Russian, which sounded like gibberish to me.

Tens of thousands of Polish Jews fled the German occupied west and started streaming east into the Russian zone in a desperate attempt to escape fresh horrors unfolding under the Nazis — The Jewish population in Lvov increased dramatically during 1940 — but many of these people decided to return to their homes and families after a few months. Life under communism was a dismal slog, and rumor had it that things had settled down in the German zone, with no mass imprisonment of Jews, no mass murder. Slowly, they began to trickle back. This infuriated Stalin. How dare these Jews reject Communism and insult the Soviet Union this way?

He established a registry for Jews to sign, ostensibly to facilitate a safe, orderly return to the west, but those who added their names were in for a nasty surprise: the NKVD, the Russian police force, stormed their houses in the middle of the night, loaded them onto trucks, forced them onto waiting trains . . . and shipped them off to Siberia. Our hearts ached for these poor souls when we heard that they'd been banished to a frozen wasteland. Little did we know, they were the lucky ones: most of them would come back alive; most of us would be slaughtered.

On June 22, 1941, after two years of living under Russian occupation, our worst fear was realized: Hitler invaded the Soviet Union and eastern Poland.

Bombs rained from the sky like hail. Everything around us seemed to be exploding and burning at once. It felt like the end of the world.

We hunkered down in the cellar of a friend's building for a couple of weeks, fifty or sixty of us crammed into a dark tight space, as the world we knew and loved was being smashed and burned to smithereens above our heads. When the building was bombed and part of it collapsed, I thought for sure we'd be buried alive. By some stroke of luck the bomb took out the side of the structure where there was no cellar.

The Russian army immediately retreated in a white-knuckled panic, which was shocking. Furiously they fled, their trucks and tanks speeding eastward along our main road — a particular target of the Nazi onslaught since it was a major supply route — careening desperately toward the Russian border, many getting blown to bits along the way. The Soviet Union had a population of over two hundred million, most of whom considered the military its crown jewel. Every day at school we had it drummed into our heads that we must at all times be prepared to wage war against "the enemies of Communism." How could the Germans overpower the mighty Russian army so easily?

We packed a few belongings and fled to Winniki, further away from the main route to Russia, to stay with my father's brother David, his wife Fay, and their children, my cousins. My parents thought that it would be safer there, less volatile. Indeed, we encountered an eerie quiet in Winniki at first. But within days the Germans exploded onto the scene, their tanks, trucks and horse troops streaming into town from all sides — an unforgettable sight. Ukrainian nationalists, foes of Russia, joined forces with the Nazis and began recruiting Jewish men and boys into forced labor, grabbing them right off the street or snatching them out of their beds.

One terrifying morning in the summer of 1941, two black-clad Ukrainian men with rubber sticks stormed into our house and dragged all the men and boys away — my uncle, father, brother, and me. We had no idea where they were taking us or if we'd come out of it alive. They dragged us to some godforsaken place and separated us, pulling Dad and me in one direction, my brother and uncle in another. Dad and I were tossed into a truck and taken to the train station, where we were ordered to unload heavy boxes of ammunition that the Russians had left behind. The place was swarming with Ukrainian police forces and German soldiers.

We didn't yet know how to tell the difference between the various branches of the German military: the SS and Gestapo (Nazi paramilitary forces), the Wehrmacht (Germany's unified armed forces), the Luftwaffe (Germany's aerial warfare division), and others. All we knew was that some of these men, whom we'd later learn were SS, were especially brutal from the start, beating us with leather straps across our hands and faces for no reason as we worked. They were base, inhuman. Who were these creeps?

Later in the day, they dragged in two more Jews, a pair of brothers named Morris and Ludwig Brandwein, bakers, neighbors of ours from Lvov, who had deserted the Russian army and were trying to get back home when they were seized. The Brandweins, young and strong, joined us in our labors. We worked for six or eight hours without a break, under terrible pressure from the SS guards who marched around with their machine guns drawn.

In the late afternoon, when no guards were about, my father and I staged a risky escape, leaping away through backyards and gardens until at last we came to my uncle's house. The Brandweins took off alongside us and headed for home. Hours later, Jozek and Uncle David made their getaway and joined us.

The whole experience left my father so sick that he decided to take us back to Lvov, even though we didn't know what was happening there. We left Uncle David's house and headed back to the old neighborhood under cover of pre-dawn darkness. As we arrived at our building we heard that some neighbors had looted our apartment while we were away. That was the least of our problems. Lvov was overrun by thousands of German tanks and military vehicles. German planes, loaded with bombs, circled overhead. We heard that there was a pogrom in our city, and that Ukrainian men, working with the SS, were killing Jews right in the street. A new law went into effect requiring that all Jews, children included, wear armbands bearing the Star of David. The penalty for disobeying this law was death.

Death. Suddenly it was everywhere.

Jewish men were seized in scores and shipped off "to work," many of them never to return, in an escalating series of so-called Akcja, or Actions. Mobs of young Ukrainian men and boys stormed through neighborhood after neighborhood, robbing and beating Jews in their homes and on the street. A gang of these blood-crazed thugs crashed into our apartment one night and dragged my father away, arresting him on a rumor that kosher butchers had been responsible for the murders at the Birgidkie jail and had sold human flesh in their shops. He was imprisoned for twenty-one days, each moment of which my mother, Jozek, Clara and I spent in the grip of a strangulating panic. He was lucky to be alive at all — these mobs usually took "justice" into their own hands. My mother scrambled frantically until finally, through a Ukrainian lawyer, friend of an old friend, she managed to arrange his release. All the others arrested alongside him were executed.

Raw barbarism was the new rule. We had no time to catch our breath.

My uncle Israel Forgenfengel and another young Jew named Chop were seized by Ukrainian nationalists and murdered sadistically, in cold blood. Israel was a gentle young man who had recently married my mother's stepsister, Sabina. Chop had a wife named Nora and a baby daughter. These were fine, intelligent boys, good-hearted souls who would never hurt a fly. The killers dragged them out to some remote location and forced them to dig a deep grave. They shot one dead and forced the other to bury him. Then they shot him, too. Even their Christian neighbors were sickened by it. But what could they do?

*Israel Forgenfengel and
his wife, Sabina*

The "movement" was spreading fast.

Ukrainian policemen took to the streets in their all-black nationalist uniforms, grave digging shovels hoisted upon their shoulders like weapons, singing a song that rings still in my ear:

"Skoro smert, skoro smert/ Smert moskowsko zydowsko comuni!"

"Early death, early death/ Early death to the Jews and Communists!"

Later that summer, nicely appointed German military vehicles filled with elegantly dressed men and women started appearing on our main road — a strange sight. These vehicles were usually reserved to transport elite fighting forces or high-ranking officials. Now they were carrying well-heeled civilians guarded by machine gun-wielding SS men. And they were headed out toward the Piaski — a large deserted area, just some old sand hills at the edge of the forest, a dead end. There was nothing there. Where were they going?

Then we heard machine gunfire.

Our neighbors ran into the street.

"Matka Boska!" they screamed. "Holy Mary! They're killing people at the Piaski!"

My mother went into the city to tell her brothers, sisters, and other relatives what was happening and warn them that the danger was spreading. They didn't believe a word of it, though they lived just mere miles away. They thought my mother was repeating wild rumors. And why shouldn't they? The scenes she described were absurd, impossible. This was the modern world. Germany was a sophisticated nation. Who could believe that genocide was upon us? This, in the end, was one of the Nazis' wiliest weapons: the sheer implausibility of it all. No one believed that a modern Western European nation was capable of this . . . and most failed to act until it was too late. But we knew what was happening. We could see it, hear it:

The Nazis were committing mass murder at the Piaski on a daily basis.

I've read many books about the Holocaust, heard many interviews with survivors and scholars, watched many movies and documentaries, but I've never seen anyone mark a specific time and place as the start of it all. Exactly when and where did the Nazi campaign of extermination begin? I contend that it was right there and then, in Lvov, at the Piaski, in the summer of 1941. Once that line had been crossed, the horrors increased a thousand fold.

That fall, a pair of Ukrainian professionals in Winniki, an attorney and an office manager, together with three SS men, issued an order that all Jewish men report to a designated place to work. When the men showed up, they were force-marched to Lesience Piaski, and executed. My Uncle David and my cousin Richard Grossman, my father's sister's boy, around my age, were among those killed. For weeks we were told that the men were working in another town and would soon return. We believed it for as long as we could.

Chapter Three

~~~

The Ukrainian attorney who had gotten my father out of jail advised my parents to move into the city and disappear. They took his advice. Aunt Bella, my mother's sister, got us a single room on the second floor of her building at 11 Kotlarska Street, in a Jewish neighborhood in the heart of Lvov, and the five of us moved in.

Jozek and I were able to get Ausweiss documents, working papers — highly sought after, issued chiefly by the SS, the Wehrmacht, or, as in our case, the Luftwaffe. We both got jobs at Sknilow Airport. Every morning we'd line up at the edge of the open Ghetto, along with several hundred other Jewish men, to get picked up by Luftwaffe soldiers and trucked out to the airfields. I was put to work on the landing pad, a dangerous assignment since the arriving planes were returning from bombing missions on the Russian front, usually badly damaged, and often crash-landed, hurting or killing people on the ground.

Aside from a cup of watery noodle soup at lunchtime, we received nothing for our labors. At least the Luftwaffe soldiers didn't whip or beat us. They were generally decent, demanding only discipline and hard work. Sometimes one of them would slip a piece of bread to one of us, glancing around nervously to make sure his comrades didn't see — Luftwaffe soldiers were largely distrustful and afraid of each other, as were SS men, and with good reason: There were many spies among their ranks.

One morning on our way to the pick-up point, the SS closed our busy street to check everyone's identification papers. My brother and I had our papers in order but an SS man hit me anyway, smashing me so hard in the face that his handprint, all five fingers, remained visible for the rest of the day.

"Du Schwein!" he sputtered. "You pig!"

I didn't understand. What had I done? Then he yelled something about my not being clean-shaven. I ran home and gave myself a fresh shave . . . as I have done every day of my life since that morning.

The SS started building fenced walls around all the Jewish neighborhoods. News spread that we would be closed in, prevented from leaving. At the same time, large numbers of people were being put to work in a factory on the grounds of a newly built "facility" on ulica Janowska, Janowska Street, in Lvov. They'd work there during the day — sewing, doing mechanics, carpentry and other jobs — and return home at night. My first cousin, Jozek Bruner, was one of these "commuters." One night, he didn't come home. Later, we learned that the SS had locked the place up and made an announcement.

"Starting today you will work here and live here," they said. "This is now your home. If you try to escape, you will be put to death. This is a concentration camp. You will be here until the end of the war."

We never saw Jozek Bruner again.

A Jewish police force was established in the open ghetto, young Jewish men who carried rubber sticks and wore badges shaped like the Star of David. One bitterly cold morning in February 1942, as my mother and I walked along ulica Kotlarska, Jewish policemen started rounding up young males to be shipped off to the Janowska Camp. Two strong, tall cops grabbed me and took hold of my arms. I tried to wriggle away but could not get free. My mother cried and begged them to let me go. They paid her no mind. As they dragged me off, we came to an area where water had spilled and frozen into a few meters of solid ice. The men tightened their grip. But I was good on the ice. Near where I grew up was a big area where water would collect and freeze every winter. My friends and I used to skate there daily and eventually became quite skilled. Now on this frozen patch of Kotlarska Street, I used those skills to save myself. I spread my feet wide across the path and tripped my captors so they fell face down on the ice. I ran thirty or forty feet away, knowing they couldn't catch me. But they grabbed my mother and shouted that they would hold her until I came to the station. Tears froze in my eyes as I warned the young men that if anything happened to my mother, I'd kill them both. They knew I meant it.

My brother urged me to appeal to a member of the Jewish Police force named Zygi, the son of a nice family who lived in our building. I knew Zygi very well and explained the situation to him, repeating that if anything bad happened to my mother, I would kill whoever was responsible. Zygi managed to convince his comrades that I meant business. The next day they let my mother go. I slept away from home for a few nights in case they decided to come for me.

The open Ghetto kept getting smaller. Another Akcja, another few thousand killed . . . and the Ghetto got smaller still. We were disappearing in droves. Those who remained were fighting sickness and starvation. It was too late to escape.

My mother and father came from families of six siblings each, all married with children, so I had lots of aunts and uncles and scores of cousins living in and around the city. Some had already been killed. Many lived close enough that we knew they were still alive. Others? We had no idea, which ate at us constantly. One day, as we sat huddled in our one-room flat, quiet as mice, trying hard to hatch some kind of plan, the front door was pushed open and in walked my cousin Lucia, followed by a Jewish policeman. We were thrilled to see her alive. Lucia ran to us and fell into our arms, weeping and unable to speak. My mother held her for a while, stroked her hair, dried her tears. What was this? What was going on?

The Jewish policeman explained that Lucia had been arrested for owning a seal coat after a deadline had passed for all Jews to surrender their fur coats and hats to the Nazis, who were ill prepared for the winter and desperately needed warm gear.

Lucia was an exceptional beauty — the Aryan ideal, as fate would have it: tall and shapely with lustrous blonde hair, luminous blue eyes, and a sparkling personality to match. Most people didn't believe she was Jewish. My mother used to tease Uncle Jack and Aunt Sally about their oldest girl's fine fair looks, wondering aloud where she possibly could have gotten them. Lucia's father, my father's brother, had died of stomach cancer in the early 1930s, leaving Aunt Sally alone to raise three young girls — Lucia, Jackie, and Stella. The family had for years owned a successful restaurant on the opposite end of town, about two hours away by public transportation, but Sally sold the place after Jack died. She started working with her cousin, a clothing manufacturer, and eventually became a well-paid buyer.

We were especially proud of Aunt Sally — it was rare in those days to see a woman as the breadwinner of the family, and a prosperous one at that.

When the order to surrender all fur clothing was issued, Sally complied. Except for the seal coat. Jack had given it to her as an anniversary gift early in their marriage and she couldn't part with it. The SS stormed the house, probably tipped off by a neighbor, found the coat, and demanded to know its owner. Desperate to save her mother and thinking, perhaps, that she'd have a better shot at survival, Lucia claimed that the coat was hers. The SS men dragged her away over Sally's shouted pleas to take her instead. I wasn't there but I can hear her voice screaming in my brain:

"It's mine! No young girl would wear such a coat! Can't you see she's lying?"

They dragged Lucia away to the notorious jail at Lackiego-Strasse, which doubled as the city's main SS headquarters, from which no prisoner ever came out alive. The SS officer in charge was immediately smitten by Lucia's incandescent beauty, the cop said, and intervened to prevent her execution. It would be a shame, he said, to waste such a pretty girl. Lucia begged him to release her. When he refused, she pleaded for a chance to see her family one last time. Amazingly, he agreed, and put this Jewish cop in charge of transporting her back and forth. Now here she was . . . but for a moment.

We surrounded the young policeman and tried everything we could to get him to let Lucia stay.

"All you have to do is disappear," I said. "Just tell them she ran away."

"You know what will happen then," he replied. "Many more will be killed in her place. And I'll be killed too."

I argued that the head officer would probably make an exception in this case. He had allowed her to be escorted out in the first place — maybe he was trying to aid her escape. Nonsense, the cop said. The boss would never take a risk like that. Getting caught saving Lucia's life could be a death sentence for him.

Mother appealed to the policeman's heart, father to his sense of morality, Jozek to his manly pride . . . all to no avail. Lucia hugged and kissed us goodbye, then let herself be led away. I don't think she said a single word the whole time, just wept and clung to us desperately until it was time to go.

That was the last time I saw her. But I see her clearly in my mind's eye even now, her face as soft and radiant as ever.

Not long after this gut-wrenching episode, in early 1942, an epidemic of typhus broke out in the Ghetto and I came down with a high fever. My parents called in a doctor who lived in our building — we had moved into another one-room flat on Zamarstynowska Street, near the bridge, in the same building as my mother's sister and her husband — and he confirmed that I'd contracted the dreaded disease. Doctors were required by law to report all such cases to the state. Failure to do so resulted in execution. All victims of typhus were immediately dispatched to one small hospital in the Ghetto. We knew what it meant to be sent there: Once the wards were all filled up, the SS would load all the sick and ailing patients onto trucks, drive them out to the Piaski, and shoot them dead.

I had no choice but to go. Luckily, I ran into a young nurse I knew from the neighborhood who promised to help if I followed her instructions exactly. She gave me a male nurse's uniform and told me to rise at five o'clock every morning and watch out the window for the SS truck. It came every ten or twelve days, depending on how full the hospital was. If I saw the truck, I was to wear the uniform and push a hospital wagon around. The SS would assume I was an employee and leave me alone. Luckily, my fever broke in a couple of days and the gentle young woman arranged my release. Two days later, the SS picked up all the sick patients and whisked them away to the Piaski.

By the middle of that same year, all remaining Jews in Lvov were required to squeeze into the Ghetto so it could be closed off and contained. Only a single gate was made available for exits and entrances. An SS guard manned the gate in a small shack and if you did not pass his scrutiny you would be taken to the Piaski and executed. We were permitted to go back and forth to work only in large groups, never alone.

Clara, ever resourceful, managed to land a factory job at Schwarz & Company, a German manufacturer of army uniforms — a highly desirable place to work, safe and reasonably stable. She made fast friends there and soon managed to get my father a job mixing cement. When the factory director asked one day if anyone had experience as a cook or butcher, my father volunteered that he was in the meat trade and had cooked for the Austro-Hungarian army during World War I. He was hired as a chef on the spot. It was like hitting the jackpot! The kitchen was the most stable, comfortable environment in the factory. Its workers could go about their business free from the constant abuse suffered elsewhere. Plus, they were surrounded by food and would never go hungry.

My father got my mother and brother jobs in the kitchen working alongside him. This was unheard of, three members of one family in the same plum spot, but they earned it with their skill and high productivity. Assisted by a sizable staff, they produced twelve hundred fifty meals a day for the daytime workers, and another twelve hundred fifty meals to be served later, to the overnight shift. The food was better under their management than it had any right to be — a nice portion of soup, a big piece of bread, and often some cheese or other treat. Sometimes people came back for a second helping. My father sneaked it to them if he could.

I had no experience in the kitchen or as a driver, so my father pulled strings to get me a job in the Receiving Department, where we took in the clothes of thousands of executed prisoners, sorted and mended them, tied them into great bundles, and tossed them onto waiting army trucks. Where they went after that I had no idea. I used to discreetly feel around for any documents or valuables possibly left in pockets or sewn into linings, but rarely found anything. The SS had thoroughly looted the clothes before sending them on to us.

My cousin Frieda and I came up with another way to squeeze some value out of my new job: I would smuggle quality garments out of the factory and we would sell them on the black market. I started coming to work lightly dressed so that I could layer other clothes underneath my own, and get them out that way. Frieda secured a relatively safe spot for us at the far end of the Ghetto, and soon we had a little side business going. We split the meager profits evenly. My parents, of course, had no idea what we were up to.

How they would have howled had they known! It was all insanely dangerous — penny-wise, pound-foolish to say the least. But our youth made us feel invincible . . . or something like it.

The factory occupied a set of four buildings that had formerly been Jewish residential apartments — 3, 5, 7 and 9 Marcina Street — and operated day and night, six days a week, staffed by two rotating shifts of workers. Each shift employed about twelve hundred fifty people overseen by four directors. Mr. Gluck, the main director, was pleasant and personable, as was his colleague, Mr. Klopotek. Rumor had it that Gluck was having an affair with a Jewish girl who worked in the office — highly verboten. The other two directors, Mr. Braun and a hunchback named Fritz, were harsh and miserable men, violent and virulently anti-Semitic.

After my brief stint in Receiving I was reassigned to the machine shop, where I learned to troubleshoot jammed or malfunctioning sewing machines — a constant problem. I was rushing off to one such assignment, clutching a toolbox in one hand and a piece of machinery in the other, when suddenly someone smashed me really hard in the face.

"Ferflucter Jude! Haben Sie nicht Respekt für die Deutschen?!"

"Filthy Jew! Have you no respect for the Germans?!"

In my haste, I hadn't noticed Director Braun walking in my direction. Protocol required that I pause, remove my cap, and bow my head reverently. When I realized my offense, I panicked and apologized profusely. This only made things worse. The sucker-punching henchman got really wild now. He struck me again in the head and roared so mightily that I thought his neck would explode.

A Jewish foreman gestured to me to stay quiet and say nothing. Everyone knew that Directors Braun and Hunchback Fritz were chummy with the NSKK, a little-known branch of the SS, which had its headquarters directly across from the factory. Were they going to deliver me into the clutches of this elite corps of murderers . . . as they had Mr. Fuchs, one of the Jewish Directors? Braun had confronted Fuchs angrily in a corridor one morning, no one knew why. A few days later, Fuchs was summoned to NSKK headquarters. He stepped inside, someone closed the door behind him, and he was shot in the back of the head. (The fact that his wife and children were allowed to live was considered no small act of mercy in our twisted universe.)

My father approached Director Braun and apologized sincerely on my behalf. Braun knew my parents well, since they ran the kitchen and he often gave them direct orders about what foods to prepare for the German officers. My father explained to Braun how embarrassed I was about my breach of protocol. I was so eager to reach and repair the broken machine that I had simply failed to see the good Director approaching.

"Please," my father implored, "say you'll forgive him."

Braun agreed. The next time I bumped into him I snatched off my mitze and bowed my head deeply. He liked this. His reptilian lips arranged themselves into something resembling a smile. Director Klopotek, Braun's gentle counterpart, was alarmed by the episode and tried to convince my parents to escape into the forest to join the Jewish and Russian resistance.

"What are you waiting for?" he asked. "For them

to take you all away?"

But the SS respected the Schwarz factory — it was, after all, the chief supplier of uniforms for the German army in the east — and its workers enjoyed a modicum of leniency. The factory even issued letter badges, R and W, to be worn at all times, signifying that we worked for the Army. We were assigned the letter W and for a while it provided a layer of protection. We were able to get jobs for a whole bunch of cousins and aunts and uncles, until a great swath of our extended family worked at the Schwarz factory.

We all lived together, each family crammed into a single small room, in a "residential complex" especially for Schwarz factory workers called City Block Housing. It was just to your left as you entered the ghetto. My sister and I worked the night shift, so we needed to sleep during daytime hours — always a challenge. From out of nowhere one day we heard a great commotion in the corridor. I stumbled out there, half asleep, to see what was going on. People were running about in a panic.

"Go look out your window!" a man screamed. "They're hanging Jewish policemen in the street!"

I raced back inside. Now Clara was awake. We looked out the window. I could not believe the scene: Nooses dangling from tree branches, streetlamps, fence posts — whatever was available — young Jewish men swinging from them by the neck, others being lined up to go next.

I got dressed in a hurry and went downstairs. Clara begged me not to but I was young and stupid and wouldn't listen. I spoke to four or five people along ulica Lokietka, where it was all happening, and each of them told me a different story about why the SS was hanging these men. Did they need a reason? That night I got so sick that I couldn't go to work. A terrible rash broke out all over my body.

"Why did you get so close to those hanged men?" my mother moaned.

She summoned a doctor who lived in our barracks and he gave me a few pills to swallow. To this day I don't know what they were, but by the next morning the rash was gone.

The Ghetto grew smaller and smaller as the Nazis continually tightened the fences around us. People were constantly being killed in the street and at the Piaski for not wearing their letter badges or for other minor infractions. We needed good news. In the early months of 1943, it came:

The Russians had stopped the German advance in Stalingrad. The war seemed to be turning around. Word spread through the Ghetto like wildfire that it would soon be over. But there was a serious downside: the defeat at Stalingrad resulted in a sudden drop in factory orders. No orders meant no work. No work meant big trouble.

I had a sweet girlfriend in those years by the name of Maryla Ober. She was around my age, shy and soft-spoken. I loved her very much. Maryla and her younger sister Irka worked on the night shift too, from eight in the evening until six in the morning. One day she and I had a disagreement over some nonsense or other, and in anger I transferred to the day shift.

Soon after, on the morning of March 30, 1943, Maryla, Irka, and over twelve hundred other workers returned to the Ghetto after their overnight shift, as usual, and were intercepted by an SS battalion with a fleet of trucks. The workers were herded onto the trucks, driven out to the Piaski . . . and executed.

Maryla, Irka, and their mother. Cousins Frieda and Helen. Cousin Jackie, Lucia's sister. Aunts and uncles by the score.

And Clara, my sister.

Our Clara.

Chapter Four

~~~

My parents aged twenty years the morning Clara was killed.

My mother sobbed and sobbed until we thought she would lose her mind, and never really recovered. Darkness consumed our lives. It felt like we were living on the crumbling lip of a canyon of grief and despair, poised to fall and keep falling forever. Clara's face and voice, her light touch, her wise and funny ways, her faithful companionship . . . her presence, her sheer presence — the loss seemed too great to bear. How would we get through this?

Clara (fourth from left, bottom row) and her Hebrew school classmates, around 1934. Every child in this picture ended up being killed by the Nazis. The teacher (center, top row) alone survived by moving to Palestine early on.

It was a welcome relief one rainy afternoon to find my old friend Bronek standing at our front door. I had no idea he was still alive. We had been close pals since childhood, as our fathers had been before us, and Bronek could always be counted on to raise a fun-filled ruckus. Now he stumbled into the apartment frightened, penniless, and utterly alone. His mother had died of cancer a few years earlier, his father recently died of typhus, the SS had killed his sister. We had to help him. How?

I had a crazy idea.

I asked my father to ask Director Gluck to allow us to bring Bronek to the factory during the daytime, as if he were a hired worker, and let him stay there at night to sleep among the maintenance men and others who lived on the grounds. To our amazement, good-hearted Gluck agreed. We brought Bronek to work with us and gave him plenty to do so he'd always look busy. He embraced his tasks cheerfully, really put his back into them. Our meager lunches were feasts to him, he'd gone hungry for so long. Bronek was a big handsome kid, over six feet tall, with a sunny personality. He quickly made a few friends, even met a girl he liked. He seemed happy. But after only a couple weeks, he whispered to me in the machine shop that he was planning to leave the factory and go into hiding in the old neighborhood. Some people were still there, he said. He could stay indoors with them during the day and sneak out at night to forage and search for a better solution.

It was insane. It was suicide. I told him so.

"Why would you leave now?" I argued. "Things are working out. Why risk it?"

But Bronek had always been stubborn.

"Just like his father," my father used to say.

I told him that Jozek and I planned to go into the forest, find a safe spot, and come back for our parents.

Soon. He should wait for us. We'd go together.

"If you want to go fast, you go alone, " I told him. "If you want to go far, you go together." I'd heard that said somewhere. Sounded right to me.

But one morning I woke up to find Bronek gone.

His timing turned out to be prophetic:

The SS stormed the factory, arrested all four directors, and announced that they were now in charge. Directors Braun and Hunchback Fritz, the viciously anti-Semitic bosses, were released soon after their arrest, but Directors Gluck and Klopotek were never heard from again. Someone must have ratted them out for having been kind and decent to us.

Then another announcement:

The Schwarz factory would be dissolved. Its workers would be transferred to Janowska Concentration Camp.

It was a death sentence.

Janowska had by then been divided into two bases — the camp itself, where the prisoners lived, and a factory, the Deutsche Ausrüstungswerke, or DAW, where they worked. A pair of notoriously cruel SS men ran the operation: Fritz Gebauer, First Commander, in charge of the DAW; and his deputy, Gustav Wilhaus, in charge of the Camp. These savage murderers hated each other almost as much as they hated the prisoners. Gebauer's sadism was legendary — it was he who gave the direct order to murder the entire night shift of Schwarz factory workers — and Wilhaus was well known to be a bloodthirsty demon. He used prisoners as target practice, shooting them at long-range from the balcony of his office, or from the front porch of his house. It was a particular pleasure of his to hand the weapon to his ten- or twelve-year old daughter so she could do the same, a perverted diversion that ended when the girl accidentally shot and wounded an SS officer.

My brother and I might be able to survive at Janowska for a few weeks if we were lucky, but my parents didn't stand a chance. We had to find a way to keep them out of there.

Jozek was a good horseman — he'd become adept at handling horse-drawn wagons back when my father still owned the butcher shop — and worked as a kutcher, or driver, for the Schwarz factory, which meant he could get around town with relative ease. Dad asked him to sneak a visit to an old friend who once worked for him in the slaughterhouse, a Polish Catholic named Misko Niedziolka, to see if Misko might help us hide until the Russians came to liberate us. We'd heard that the Russians were putting up a good fight against the Germans, making steady westbound progress — our best hope.

The next day, in his factory-issued horse and wagon, Jozek took a dangerous detour to Misko's house in Krzywczyce, not far from Lvov. Misko eagerly promised to help, saying that his brother, a poor farmer, could secure a good hiding place for my parents far from the village. When Jozek returned with this unbelievably good news, we felt something like happiness for the first time in years. All he and I wanted was for our parents to survive, and vice versa. We dared hope that with Misko's help and a little luck, survival might be possible for all of us.

The deadline loomed for the closing of the Schwarz factory. Jozek and the other drivers were ordered to transport a certain number of people out to the camp each day, along with sewing machines, textiles, tables, and all types of other equipment. A couple named Mr. & Mrs. Eisenberg committed suicide rather than be taken to the camp, which was becoming commonplace. The Eisenbergs, like so many others, had swallowed zyankali, a popular instant poison that had to be sourced very carefully as many hucksters sold fake concoctions. An SS man named Caulke, a kind soul who never did us any harm, happened to be on duty on the day of the Eisenberg suicide, and arranged for a proper Jewish burial on factory grounds. It is probably still there today.

An SS commander named Grzymer issued an order requiring all Jewish men to shave their heads so they could easily be spotted outside the Ghetto. I had a nice head of hair, the preferred style for young men of the day, and loathed the thought of losing it. After the deadline for head shaving had passed, the SS and the Jewish Police stationed themselves at the Ghetto gates and pulled out all the men who had not complied. A few SS men yanked me out of a column of people one morning and told me to lie down on the ground. They handed a whip to a Jewish policeman, a young man I knew pretty well, and ordered him to beat me. He did so, but gently. The SS men became enraged. They let me go and put the policeman in my place, saying that they would show him how to whip a Jew. I ran away in a sick panic, relieved to have escaped a beating but tormented by the hideous sounds that followed: The crack of the whip against the young man's back, his anguished screams — over and over again. Over my shoulder I thought I saw a couple of SS men coming after me. Were my eyes playing tricks? I darted down one alley and then another until I felt I had shaken them.

The clock was running down for us. We had to get my parents to safety.

Good Misko had secured a hiding place, but the problem remained of how to get them there in one piece.

My father appealed to an old friend for help, a Ukrainian policeman named Grzesko, an easy-going fellow who used to drop by the factory kitchen to sample little treats my mother prepared especially for him. He'd always shown our family genuine kindness and concern, and agreed without hesitation to sneak my parents out of the city and get them safely past the most dangerous zones. Grzesko instructed them to dress like Ukrainian peasants and be ready to leave on a certain Thursday evening after eight o'clock. They would make the dangerous journey of over six kilometers on foot. My parents had managed to stash away some money — over twenty thousand zloty, equivalent to about the same amount in dollars. Dad gave five thousand each to Jozek and me, and divided the remaining ten thousand between my mother and him in case they got separated.

So that was our plan: Mom and Dad would go into hiding; Jozek and I would be put to work at the Janowska DAW, escape at the first opportunity, and join them. I knew that when we arrived at the Camp we would be forced to relinquish all our belongings — if you tried to conceal anything, no matter how small, you would be shot instantly — so I gave my share of the cash to Jozek. As a driver, he had the right to sleep in the hayloft, among the horses, and could easily hide it there.

On the appointed evening, with my parents donned in Ukrainian garb, Grzesko arrived wearing his trademark smile, wide and toothy. He told my parents that he would talk loudly to them in Ukrainian. They were to remain silent, only occasionally answering "tak," Ukrainian for "yes." My parents bade us a tearful goodbye and went on their way.

We counted the minutes until the next night. Grzesko didn't show up at first and we feared the worst . . . but then he appeared again with that smile, eyes sparkling. All was well. He told us that he'd worn civilian clothes on the journey to call less attention to himself, and carried a loaded gun in his pocket, just in case. About halfway to their destination, he and my parents were stopped by a pair of uniformed Ukrainian policeman. Grzesko, keeping my parents a good distance behind him, told the cops that these good people were leading him to a secret place where Jews were hiding. They seemed unconvinced. Grzesko tried instead to bribe them. He knew that if they refused the five hundred zloty he offered, he'd have to kill them both. They hesitated for a moment, then took the money and disappeared. Grzesko walked my parents the rest of the way along a quiet country road until at last they came to the village of Krzywczyce. There, he kissed them goodbye, wished them luck, and jumped on a slow train back to the city.

My parents were safe. At least for now.

Chapter Five

~~~

By the end of April 1943, a few weeks after the Schwarz factory murders, the Ghetto was nearly deserted. Most people had already been transported to the Janowska Camp; soon it would be Jozek's and my turn to join them. On one of my last mornings in that eerie ghost town, I spotted a young man kicking a soccer ball in the street, a strange sight. I noticed that the kid had a professional flair to his playing, and as I got a closer look I nearly fainted. It was Blatt, top goalie on Hasmonea, the Jewish soccer team, one of the best players in Poland. I could barely contain my excitement. Soon, a few other boys appeared, from where I don't know, and we started kicking the ball around. Suddenly, I was playing soccer with one of my idols! If only my friends were alive to see this! Who would I brag to?

No sooner had I begun to lose myself in this rare pleasure than a truck appeared on the road, and came screeching to a halt just yards away. Eight or nine SS men jumped off the back and started running at us. There was no time to react — Blatt and I were finished. I understood in a flash that this would be my last day, last hour, last few moments of life. What would my parents do now? How would Jozek fare without me at his side?

But then the SS officers, young men in their early twenties, took off their shirts and started kicking the ball around with us. Unbelievable. They were excellent players, but we engaged them cautiously; we knew that any small mishap could turn this bizarre game into an instant death sentence. We played for a while, and then the young men simply put their shirts back on, hopped back onto the truck, and drove away, waving at us as they disappeared. Blatt and I looked at each other for a long moment, then broke out laughing. No one would ever believe this.

A day or so later, Jozek and I were ordered to report to Janowska to join the other prisoners. We passed through the ghastly gates in silence, and were separated immediately. Jozek would continue to work as a driver, even here at Janowska, a job with substantial benefits: Not only would he still to be able to move about the city, but he and the other drivers would be permitted to sleep in the stable, among the horses. It was a far better living arrangement than the filthy, stinking, jam-packed bunker in which I was housed. It was dark and unbearably hot, and my "mattress" was a rough wooden plank placed way up high, one of many such multi-tiered "bunk beds."

Here at the DAW, I would no longer be a sewing machine mechanic but a presser, ironing uniforms for the German army ten or twelve hours a day or more. We had an hour for lunch, but the kitchen was on the opposite end of the camp so getting there and back took up a good chunk of that time. On my first day, I took one look at the long line of workers waiting to eat while a crazy-eyed SS man paced back and forth, waving his gun, and decided to skip it. By the next day, the need to eat was overwhelming. I joined the line.

During one such wretched lunchtime, the SS dragged in some captives from the city; Jewish men, women, and children who had been posing as Christians, led them onto a nearby hill, and shot them dead right in front us as we ate our soup and bread.

As bad as it was in the open Ghetto, and later in the closed Ghetto, it was nothing compared to this. Daily mass executions, six days a week, were the rule here. Only on Sundays did the killing cease. Many of my fellow prisoners had given up in their hearts and just wanted it to be over with. Why endure this unbearable life when sudden death was just around the corner?

New transports arrived almost every day from surrounding towns and villages, most of whom were taken straight to the Piaski and shot. We usually knew where these people had come from since the SS would tell the Jewish Police force, and some of them, in turn, would tell us. News and information traveled quickly from prisoner to prisoner — what to avoid, how to be extra careful in different circumstances, and so on. Above all, everyone agreed, it was important to look clean, young, and strong at all times. This much, at least, became easy for Jozek and me since we soon had plenty to eat. He was able to smuggle in good stuff like salami, butter, cheese, fresh rolls. When the food was too much to eat at one time, I'd hide it between stacks of extra clothing and blankets in the basement storage room of the building in which I worked. To be caught doing this would mean instant death.

And then one day it happened.

I had just eaten half a salami sandwich and stashed the other half between some work clothes, and was heading back up the u-shaped basement steps. I had tears in my eyes — my head and heart were in a terrible state that day. I had come to doubt the chances of our survival. The horror I was witnessing on a daily basis was crushing me from the inside out. As I gathered myself, stepped up onto the landing, and walked back into the pressing room, the entrance doors flew open and there stood Fritz Gebauer, First Commander, flanked by four SS men.

The lizard-eyed lowlife glared at me and asked why I was crying. Shaken but thinking fast, I answered that I had eine zahnschmerzen, a toothache. I covered my mouth, fearing that he would smell the salami and discover my stash. He glanced around the pressing room, looked me up and down. I was sure that my life was about to end. My fondest hope in that moment was to be killed quickly and not tortured.

"Shoot me now," I thought. "Don't drag it out."

What was he doing here anyway? Fellow prisoners had filled my head with advice for dealing with Gebauer and Wilhaus — how best to survive under their rule, how to behave if I ever found myself in their presence, how to avoid having that happen in the first place, and so on — but no one had suggested that either man would actually show up in shops and workplaces unannounced. It was simply unheard of, as far as I knew. Was this a new offensive? Was I about to become its first victim?

Gebauer glared at me for a long moment — I made it a point to be clean-shaven and well-groomed at all times, ever since that Nazi slapped me on the street for having stubble on my chin — then winked to the SS men and moved on, allowing me to live. It was an uncommon act of mercy, the only one I would ever witness from this man, a rare exception. It would not be repeated. Later that day I hurried back down to the basement, rounded up all the smelly foodstuffs, discreetly smuggled them to the outdoor toilet, and tossed them into the filthy pit ten feet deep or more. I told Jozek not to bring me any more outside food, or at least not any with a strong smell.

A good number of Polish Catholics also worked at Janowska, especially at the DAW, but not as prisoners. They'd arrive early in the morning, work until five or six o'clock, and then go home again. We were relieved to discover a dear old friend among this group: a Polish Catholic fellow named Staszko Czudowski, one of the nicest people we'd ever known. He was friendly with many of the folks from the old days … including Misko Niedziolka. We asked him to find out from Misko how our parents were doing. A few days later, he smuggled us a letter written in my mother's own hand.

Joy! She wrote that she and my father were safely hidden in a good place, that Jozek and I should come as soon as possible, and that we could bring an extra person with us since there was room for one more. I arranged for Staszko to meet me that Friday so I could give him a letter to take back to my parents in which I wrote that Jozek and I would come hajom muhor, really soon. I prayed it would prove true. Staszko met me at the appointed place and I carefully passed him the letter. Had we been discovered, we'd have been killed on the spot.

Jozek came to me a few mornings later — it was late June, we'd been prisoners for about two and half months by then — and told me to drop everything and follow him. He was going to break us out with his two-horse drawn wagon. We would get through the SS gate with our passirshein — he had managed to get me listed as an assistant driver so we both had proper papers — travel to the edge of the city, abandon the horse and wagon, disappear into the cornfields, and run. Just run. He had a good idea where my parents were hiding, he said. With a little luck, we would find them.

It worked! We got through the gate without incident. But as we headed down Janowska Street we saw something strange: the SS, Gestapo, and Ukrainian police were standing at attention everywhere, armed with machine guns. What was this? Jozek had never seen anything like it on any of his routine trips to the city. Something was wrong.

A trolley car conductor told us that Heinrich Himmler himself, Chief Commander of the SS, was visiting today on an inspection tour. Jozek looked at me with dread in his eyes. It was too dangerous. We had to go back. We returned to Janowska with sick hearts, deeply dejected to pass through those hellish gates once more, but fiercely determined to try again at a safer time.

Hajom muhor. Soon, really soon.

Chapter Six

~~~

By the time we got back to camp, everyone knew that Himmler was on his way. Rumor had it that he and Wilhaus were old friends from the heimland, Germany. Himmler had visited the camp several times before ... and his visits were always followed by a great slaughter.

We had to get out.

In my entire stay at Janowska I encountered only one prisoner I knew from the old neighborhood, a quiet, scholarly man named Nathan Schrank. Everyone else had been murdered. Schrank's wife was among the dead, but he had a daughter named Dora who was in hiding at the home of a good Christian family. I told him that my parents were in hiding, too, and that Jozek and I were planning to escape and join them. I offered him to come with us but he didn't want to risk it. He was trying to secure a hiding place close to his daughter. He was making arrangements, he said, just waiting to confirm them.

I never saw Nathan Schrank alive again.

Jozek and I felt that we should not let my mother's offer of an extra place in hiding go to waste. Henek Hauben, a lanky young man from a small town east of Lvov, leapt hungrily at the chance to take Nathan Schrank's place. Henek's wife and five-year old daughter had already been killed ... along with his parents and entire extended family.

Early one morning, just days after our first

escape attempt, Jozek came to the pressing room and whispered that I should not go to lunch. We would stage another escape attempt that day, he said, and I needed to stay nearby. He resurfaced a few hours later, just before noon, and motioned for me to follow him outside toward a waiting truck. Henek was already sitting in the back. I hopped up and joined him. Jozek climbed in next to the driver, a good Christian friend of his whose name I have lost to time but in whose debt I shall always remain. This gentle young man had nothing to gain by helping us, and everything to lose. He knew what he was risking. He risked it willingly.

We approached the gate at about eleven fifty-five in the morning, just moments before lunchtime and the changing of the guard. Jozek and the driver had planned our escape exactly this way, knowing that the guards did not like any delays during such times and would often wave drivers through perfunctorily. Just as we hoped, the SS men on duty glanced briefly at our passirshein and gave us the signal to pass.

We rolled through the gates and out of Janowska. Away, away.

Henek and I started to strip off our Star of David patches, leaving them attached by just a thread. We wanted to rip them off completely but knew we mustn't — they justified our presence in the truck as Jewish prisoners. Jozek directed the driver on a route through the city and out toward the countryside, until, before long, we came to a quiet road south of Lvov, bordered on one side by rows of corn at full height. The truck stopped alongside a stretch of railroad tracks that ran parallel to the road, and Jozek jumped out. He told Henek and me to do the same. We thanked the driver, crossed the tracks, and disappeared into the cornfields.

Just because we didn't see anybody didn't mean we hadn't been seen. We hunkered down inside the cornfield and peered through the tall stalks to make sure we were alone, then trudged further in. It was about an hour past noon, so the heat was brutal — the summer of '43 burned hotter than any I can remember, or maybe it just seemed that way. We sat quietly for a long time, tucked into the rows of corn, waiting for cover of night before we ventured any further. We had a couple of slices of bread and salami, no water. Our tongues puckered in our heads. In my life, time would never go so slowly as it did that day.

Recalling how my father had always taken care to give us each a stash of money in case we got separated, I asked Jozek for the five thousand zloty he was holding for me. He flashed me a guilty look and blurted out a series of words that scalded my ears:

"I lost it in a card game. Mine too."

This was a catastrophe. How could my brother do this to us? Without a few zlotys, we would not survive. I didn't know if my parents had any money left, assuming we'd be able to reach them at all. How would we tell them that the money was gone? I prayed that Henek had some cash but couldn't bring myself to ask. Jozek looked down, looked away, waited for the moment to pass. I was upset to the point of numbness. I didn't know how I would ever forgive him.

Suddenly, out of nowhere, we heard a man's voice singing. We peered through the tops of the corn and saw a farmer cutting stalks with his mighty kosy — a wide blade nearly a yard long, razor sharp — and tossing the harvest into a horse-drawn wagon. We froze, trapped, too close to move without being detected. The area the farmer was clearing was not very wide. He'd reach us in minutes. His song was a popular anthem of Ukrainian nationalism, rife with vicious anti-Semitism. This man would kill us without a thought. Closer and closer he came with his hate-filled song, swinging his blade, felling corn.

"Use it," I whispered to Jozek, pointing to a bagnet that had been smuggled to him by the driver. "Kill him!"

He faltered, tried to hand me the weapon. "You do it."

"You're stronger," I urged. "Kill him before he kills us."

Jozek went silent for a moment. "I can't," he said.

I turned to Henek. Henek looked away.

"Then I'll do it," I said in a panic, my heart pounding madly. "You hold him."

I took the bagnet from Jozek. The farmer came closer. I raised the vicious blade and steadied myself. I would kill this man in cold blood, the price of survival.

All at once, the skies darkened and a heavy rain began to fall. The farmer left the field. And the whole ordeal was over.

Tears flew from Jozek's eyes.

"My G-d did this for us," he said.

We remained hunkered down in that same spot until nightfall, soaked to the bone but relieved and grateful.

It was a moonless night, pitch black. Jozek led us along a route where there were almost no homes. Here and there dogs barked in our direction, but we passed otherwise undetected until we arrived, at last, at the village of Krzywczyce, where Misko Niedziolka lived with his family. The house was in the middle of town with many neighbors close by, so it was too dangerous for the three of us to approach as a group. Jozek left Henek and me to hide in some bushes and went on alone.

Time passed. No Jozek.

Maybe he got arrested. Or killed. What would we do? Henek and I didn't know this area, didn't know where Misko lived. We had no money, no food. Just when I'd begun to believe he was gone for good, Jozek came stealing back with Misko in tow. The two of them led us back toward the house in stealthy silence.

Babcia Niedziolka, Misko's mother, hid us in a pitch-black room and brought us hot coffee and bread and butter. We stayed there a good while — Misko didn't want to risk trekking out to his brother's farm, the hiding place, until the deep of night. Later, as we prepared to leave, he said we shouldn't travel in a group but trail each other by a distance of five or six meters. We trekked this way for an hour or more, a desperate four-man caravan, through forest and open country, and eventually came upon a farm with a big old shack. Dogs barked as we approached. It was hard to believe that my mother and father were just on the other side of those thin walls.

As Misko opened the door and we stepped inside, time stood still.

Chapter Seven

~~~

My parents became hysterical when they saw us. We embraced and wept and held each other for what seemed like hours.

They welcomed Henek, a stranger, as their own, and we all stayed up until the early morning to talk about the living hell we'd seen at Janowska. Staszek and Katarzyna Niedziolka, our hosts, Misko's brother and his wife, were warm and friendly people, so kind and accommodating.

Their house was basically a two-room shack with an earthen floor. The main room consisted of a large kitchen, a single window, a bed, and not much else. A smaller room, crudely attached, contained a long, pallet-style bedding arrangement in which the

Katarzyna and Staszek Niedziolka

Niedziolka children lay sleeping in a neat row . . . all five of them! Young as I was, only eighteen, I nearly had a heart attack at the sight. How would our secret survive with all these children running about? (A sixth child, the oldest boy, lived in town with Babcia, his grandmother.)

By early morning, it was time for sleep. My father led us through a little door in the kitchen, maybe three-by-two, that led to a passageway so narrow that we had to bend deeply, nearly crawl, in order to get through. The passageway opened onto a humble stable used to house straw and hay . . . and a lone milking cow. A hole in the ceiling in a corner of the stable led to the cramped attic, our hiding place. The five of us climbed up, using a piece of wood nailed to the wall for footing. The attic was on a sharp pitch and had low ceilings, perhaps four feet at the highest point, so we couldn't stand upright. Mother arranged some blankets and we settled in.

At Janowska, I slept very little. The heat was brutal and my narrow, splintered bunk was placed so high up that I was always afraid of falling. Besides, my mind raced constantly with fantasies of escape. I'd toss and turn in a feverish state, flinching at every sound, wondering about my parents, praying that Jozek was safe in the stable. Now, in this low-slung attic deep in the Polish countryside, I slept and slept and slept, rarely waking up before noon for the first month or so. Our loving protector, Katarzyna, who we called Kasia, brought us hot meals every day — boiled potatoes with onion and gravy, strong coffee with saccharine. Mother would split the food between us and serve according to our ages, oldest first.

Jozek and I wondered quietly to each other whether it would be possible to survive in this place. It was reasonably remote, but people dropped by for various reasons almost everyday, so even an ill-timed cough or sneeze could give us away. (We kept a special rag on hand to muffle such noises.) And then there were the children: the oldest, Józka, a beautiful girl of sixteen; Vladek, thirteen; Broner, twelve; Zosia, ten; and the baby, Romek, three. We took care during waking hours to stay at the far end the attic, away from the front of the house, so as not to draw their attention, and even changed our names in case the children ever uttered them in public.

My father become Uncle Misko, my mother Aunt Vikto, Henek became Broner, I became Kazik, and Jozek remained Jozek — all familiar names in the Niedziolka family, which we hoped would confuse matters and give us some cover.

The attic was roofed in red terra cotta tiles with little spaces between them through which we could get a clear view of the outside, a valuable feature. But there was a downside: these tiles baked in the summer sun from dawn to dusk, heating the attic like an oven, roasting us, suffocating us. We asked Kasia to pass up buckets of water so we could drink and sponge ourselves off but it provided little relief. Despite the abject misery of our circumstances, we were happy to be together and grateful to this kind and generous family. Staszek (or Staszko, as we called him), Kasia, and their children — along with my family, Henek, and I — would all be executed if discovered. The risk they were taking was insane.

At sundown, after things cooled off a bit, Kasia would usually pass up a big salad of tomatoes, cucumbers, onions, potatoes, along with loaves of bread. In the late evenings, after nine or ten o'clock, we'd climb down to stretch our legs and talk to our hosts. The Gestapo had imposed a nightly curfew of eight o'clock and no one dared defy it, so it was usually safe for us to be outdoors without the danger of neighbors or others happening by. Two dogs roamed the property. They were valuable assets that could sense people approaching from far away. I loved and treasured those hounds for the measure of security they provided our family, but, still, our safety was fragile at best.

From the earliest days of my arrival at the farm, I heard constant machine gunfire coming from the Piaski — just a couple of kilometers away, separated from us only by a small village called Maly Krzywczyce. During my thirteen months in hiding at the Niedziolka farm, from June 1943 to July 1944, tens of thousands of people were slaughtered there, maybe more — men, women and children, Jewish prisoners from Janowska, refugees from the pogroms in Lvov and Winniki, Russians, others. The near constant executions could be heard for miles around, striking terror even in the hearts of the Gentile population. Soon, a vile odor began to permeate the attic. It got under our noses, turned our stomachs, kept us awake at night. My mother scrubbed, my father filled cracks with strips of cloth, all to no avail. What was this foul stench? Finally, from Staszko, we found out: The Death Brigade had come to town.

Also known as the 1005th Brigade, this band of about a hundred fifty Jewish prisoners, strong young men, were stationed in a special bunker at the Piaski and charged with the unspeakable task of exhuming and cremating the corpses of hundreds of thousands of murdered Jews, Russian POWs, Gypsies and others — even as mass killings continued at the Piaski on regular basis. The Death Brigade was dispatched daily, under SS supervision, to dig up mass graves all over the countryside, transport the rotting corpses back to the Piaski, stack the corpses on pyres of specially-formulated quick-burning wood, douse them with tar and petrol, and incinerate them. Massive fire pits were also used for the same purpose. The Nazis were destroying evidence, pure and simple.

It didn't matter which way the wind blew. The stench of burning rotting flesh was everywhere. It scalded our eyes, scorched our noses and throats, filled our breasts and bellies with rage, revulsion, heartbreak, panic. The fires were burning just a stone's throw away from where my family had lived for generations. The Nazis installed a special bone-grinding machine — basically a big cement mixer with a couple of cannonball like orbs inside — to pulverize the charred remains into dust, the dust to be used as fertilizer in the same fields from which we had eaten for all those years.

None of this was any secret to the Gentile villagers. Whether or not they were bothered by it, I'll never know.

We knew that there were plenty of others like us, Jews in hiding with friends or neighbors, many of whom had paid out large sums of money for the favor — always a dangerous affair. Many unscrupulous people would take money . . . then call the Gestapo anyway. Others would accept money on a long-term promise, but grow tired or scared and chase their charges away too soon. In the city, the dangers were magnified. Streets and buildings were densely packed and people were so nosy that they'd peek into a neighbor's pot to see what was on for dinner. Plenty of these same people were actively seeking out Jews to hand over to the Gestapo in exchange for a paltry reward.

My parents gave Staszko all the money they had when they first arrived, the equivalent of about ten thousand dollars. Big mistake. He burned through it so quickly that by the time Jozek, Henek and I arrived, it was almost gone. My father asked Jozek and me to kick in our stashes and was horrified to learn that Jozek had gambled it all away. Henek jumped immediately to the rescue: He pulled out an old cloth bag and opened it to reveal a stash of twenty-dollar gold pieces. Now I understood why Jozek had asked him to escape with us! It was a miraculous moment. I don't know how we would have survived without it. And I still don't know how Henek managed to hide the gold all that time.

At Janowska we were marched by the SS to the bathhouse every couple of weeks in groups of several hundred for entlausing, or delousing, forced to sing the hideous concentration camp song, "Bośmy Chłopcy Jacy" along the way (it translates roughly as "We're Just Good Ol' Boys"). We showered naked, under close supervision — in extremely hot water with plenty of lye soap to kill lice and other parasites — so Henek couldn't have concealed anything on his person. He couldn't have sewn the gold coins into his clothing, either, since we regularly surrendered our clothes and shoes for disinfection and rarely, if ever, got the same set back. And it was far too dangerous to hide anything in the barracks. So how had he done it? I still don't know. He said something about moving it around all the time — much harder than it sounds. In any event, thank G-d he pulled it off: That gold was key to our continued survival.

Henek gave Staszko one piece every few weeks to sell on the black market. Staszko I can only compare to an angel, so good and kind ... but not too sharp. We had to coach him closely on the dangers of trading in the black market — Gestapo agents posing as civilians,

civilians working secretly as informants, and so on. On the morning he left to make the first sale, we held our breath. By nightfall he was home again, proudly displaying a small bundle of cash. That bought us a little more time. But how much?

It was expensive to feed five extra mouths. And dangerous. Shopping for provisions in unusually large quantities could arouse suspicion. We coached Staszko not to shop in the nearby village of Krzywczyce, but to travel to Lvov instead. We told him to buy from a variety of local farmers, not the same ones all the time, and to avoid unknown merchants. We designed roundabout travel routes so he would be less likely to be seen by familiar people. We suggested that Kasia do some shopping too, always in a different neighborhood.

I never stopped fearing that the Niedziolka children would eventually blow our cover, but they were so sweet and helpful that I grew quite fond of them. In a very short time, our two families came to feel like one. Our old pal Misko came to visit from time to time with updates about the Russian advance. Babcia, his and Staszko's mother, often joined him, always bringing delicious cakes, coffees and other goodies, or even fully cooked meals with all the trimmings. Babcia is Polish for Grandma . . . and this supremely kind woman lived up to every ounce of the warmth and goodness the name implies.

"She's a rare diamond," my parents would say. And she was.

She spoke often about a young boy who scrounged around her neighborhood at night in search of food and water. His name was Izio Krimsztok, she told us, the youngest child of successful Jewish merchants and property owners from Krzywczyce. His entire family had been murdered. Now he spent his days hiding in haystacks and coal bins, venturing out only after sundown. Babcia gave him food, clothing, and other supplies whenever she could, but thoughts of him kept her awake at night. How would he survive like this, all alone?

Babcia spoke so vividly and tenderly about the boy that we felt we knew him, felt he was one of our own. Something had to be done. My family and I mulled over all the options, then suggested to Babcia that she take Izio into hiding with the understanding that he would reward her with a piece of his family's property when the war was over . . . if they survived. Babcia seemed hesitant to extract such a promise but we argued that she was entitled to it. Wouldn't she be risking her life to hide him? He'd be happy and grateful to repay her this way, we said, and we knew firsthand it was true. Babcia agreed. She approached Izio one night and made the offer. He pounced on it eagerly, as we knew he would, and was promptly installed in a hidden trench inside Babcia's horse stable. It was a high-risk arrangement with so many neighbors around, but at least Izio would be protected from the elements and filled with good food and drink. We all slept better knowing that.

Babcia's house was made of brick, nicely built, with a pair of strong horses, a couple of cows, and a good plot of land for growing fruits and vegetables. When she and her husband had gotten "divorced" many years earlier — not officially, as the Catholic Church forbade it — she "adopted" her grandson Kazik (again, unofficially) and raised him as her own. A few years after that, she took in a Ukrainian orphan named Michael from east of Lvov. She raised Michael as a son and taught him to handle horses, cattle, and all farm-related business. She thought the world of him, even promising that when he got married she would sign some of her land over to him and his new bride. Their relationship was especially poignant in that Poles and Ukrainians had little love for each other in those days.

Though Babcia always spoke of "her boys" in glowing terms, especially Michael — it was he who dug the hidden trench for Izio — my parents urged her to keep our existence a secret from them. The fewer people who knew about us the greater our chances of survival. But it was not to be.

Michael popped up unexpectedly one day and discovered my brother standing in the middle of the stable with nowhere to hide. Jozek had climbed down for only a moment, I forget why, and left the opening exposed . . . so the rest of us were clearly visible, too. Michael's eyes met ours for a long, tense moment. No one spoke or even breathed. Then he smiled, greeted us warmly, kissed us like family, and vowed to help in every way.

This beautiful man quickly became our treasured friend and ally, visiting often, bringing good cheer and, more importantly, newspapers. The daily Gazeta Lwowska was like gold to us, as was the German paper, the Lemberger Zeitung. But it was dangerous for Stasko or Kasia to pick them up: humble farm folk didn't read newspapers (or anything else), so buying them could easily arouse suspicion. Staszko risked it from time to time, traveling to far reaches of the city to buy the papers anonymously, but these occasions were rare. Michael changed all that. He was clever and fearless and fed us a steady supply of fresh newsprint. Some of what we read gave us hope: The Russians and Americans were making solid headway.

Michael, Babcia's adopted son

Henek gathered us all together one October morning — we'd been in hiding for almost four months by then — and said he had something important to discuss. His good friend Falik was hiding in the storage warehouse of a textile business for which his girlfriend Halina, a Gentile, worked as a manager. He lived there "like a mouse," Henek said, crawling among the boxes, eating only when Halina was able to sneak in some food, cowering in fear whenever workers passed through. Halina was a highly educated counter-revolutionary, one of many Russian expats living in the German zone who openly rejected communism. The Nazis viewed such people favorably, so Halina had many German friends and co-workers. The situation was too close, too hot. Henek asked if we would agree to let Falik join us here in the attic. If so, he'd ask the Niedziolkas for their blessing.

How do you say no to such a request? Yet the word "yes" stuck like a bone in my throat.

As much as you'd like to help save another man's life, even a stranger's, you don't want to risk more than a dozen other lives in the process. I argued against it strongly. Falik's hiding place was a good distance away, at least ten kilometers or more, and the journey from there to the Niedziolka farm would have to be made by foot — it was too dangerous to risk it any other way. Henek had mentioned that Falik looked and sounded very Jewish. Any nosy passer-by would become suspicious in an instant. How would he, and whoever guided him here — probably Staszko — manage to avoid being captured, tortured, and forced to give up our whereabouts? How would Staszko explain to friends and strangers why he was traveling on foot? What would he say when they offered to give him a ride? The whole thing sounded crazy, it scared me to death. I urged my parents to refuse. But in the end they felt we had to say yes. Henek spoke to Staszko and Kasia and they, too, gave their blessing.

Staszko and Kasia: Either they were unaware of how great the danger was ... or their essential goodness and generosity knew no bounds.

We devised a plan: Henek would write a letter to Halina explaining everything, which Staszko would deliver to her by hand. At an appointed day and time, Staszko would meet Falik, lead him out of the city and through the forest on foot, and bring him to the hiding place. They wouldn't walk together in public, or even acknowledge each other. Many people were paid to roam the city streets and spot situations just like this, and they were quite good at it. The only thing we had in our favor was that it was October, so the skies went dark early.

Jozek and I calculated the time the trip would take — about sixty or seventy minutes from the city to the forest, and about thirty minutes through the forest to the farm — not more than an hour and forty minutes altogether. We never mentioned it to my parents, but we planned to force them to flee with us into the forest if Staszko and Falik failed to appear inside of two hours.

The day arrived. Staszko set out. We crouched quietly in the attic, breathing in shallow gulps, staring through the roof tiles in the direction from which the men would arrive. Tick-tock, tick-tock. Time seemed literally to crawl.

And then, at around eight o'clock, the dogs started to bark. Staszko emerged from the woods. Behind him, at a distance of maybe six meters, loped a tall man in a too-small woolen jacket, rangy and gangly, all arms and legs.

This was Falik Weiser, our new bunkmate.

Chapter Eight

~~~

We showed Falik how to hoist himself up into the attic. My mother served him some food she'd set aside and we gathered around as he ate, hungry for stories of the outside world. But Falik was exhausted. He collapsed into a makeshift bed and fell into a deep slumber. In the morning, all he wanted to talk about was Halina, his Gentile girlfriend, for whom he'd abandoned his wife.

They'd been living together in Lvov for a few months when the Germans invaded. Halina had been brutal to him during his time in hiding, he said, berated him for being a Jew, threatened to expose him, made him go for long periods without food.

"How can you get involved with a woman like that?" my mother asked. "You left a wife in Krakow. When this war is over, if she survives, you'll come to your senses and go back to her."

"I'll go back to my wife," Falik responded darkly. "But first I will kill Halina."

My mother looked at us, bemused.

"He'll never go back to his wife. And he'll never kill this woman. If he survives, it's to her he'll run." She was usually right about such things.

Falik was a huge man, over six feet tall, and consumed giant portions of food. We asked Kasia for more but she was already spreading the rations thin. We all quietly resented our new bunkmate's ravenous hunger, gangly body, brooding eyes. We resented his arrogance, his demanding nature. He seemed to expect special privileges and considerations — I don't know what he thought we could do for him up in that tiny attic. Falik never talked about his parents and siblings, or the wife he'd left behind. His only topic of conversation all day, everyday, was Halina . . . and the various ways he might kill her. Had bringing him here been a terrible mistake?

Winter approached. A bitter cold settled into the attic . . . and our bones. It effected the way we held our bodies — limbs wrapped around ourselves; the way we breathed — always a thin film of steam blossoming from our mouths; the way we slept — very little. I remember wincing as my mother shook icicles out of my hair.

We never thought we'd be in hiding this long. According to the newspapers, the Germans were losing the war on all fronts. They'd made a few key miscalculations, lacked sufficient supplies to survive the winter, and were running out of clothing, gas, ammunition, food, blankets, everything. They'd already lost several hundred miles of territory. Yet the war raged on. The days grew colder.

We decided to build a bunker underground — a daunting project, since we had neither the tools nor skills required, but critical to our continued survival. A bunker would provide greater insulation from the icy temperatures and ensure that the six of us — mother, father, Henek, Falik, Jozek and I — would be more securely hidden.

We chose a site located on the side of the house near the stable entrance. Jozek, Michael, Kasia and I trekked deep into the forest under cover of night to scout for nice strong trees to cut, strip and drag home as lumber, hiding the frozen planks inside the house until they were needed. Michael, bless him, brought us sheets of tar to use as insulation and a horse-drawn wagon to help with the heavy lifting. He brought his sturdy back, skilled hands, willing heart.

It took several days to build the bunker. We worked only during midnight hours, and masked the worksite with shrubbery as best we could in the daytime.

In pretty short order we managed to build a sizable bunker of about fifty square feet, strong and solid. Michael, Jozek, and I dug a narrow tunnel connecting the bunker to the stable and installed a trap door right underneath Staszko's cow so we could slide in and out undetected . . . once the old heifer moved out of the way.

Our underground hideout was a tight fit for the six of us, but much warmer than the attic. It was only about three feet high at its tallest point, so there was barely enough headroom to sit upright. All we could do was hunker down in a tight cluster. Staszko gave us a kerosene lamp so we wouldn't live in total darkness. When the fumes got too intense we'd extinguish the lamp and stare into blackness.

The space was too tiny to allow for a toilet area, so we had to control our bodily functions until those rare moments when someone would open the bunker door so we could relieve ourselves in a corner of the stable. Sometimes, in an emergency, if it was late and quiet enough, we'd let ourselves out for this purpose. It was very risky since we couldn't see what was happening outside, and we'd usually have to push and push at the trapdoor to shake the old cow off it — it seemed to be her favorite spot — and this created an unwelcome commotion.

Kasia continued to send in hot coffee and regular

meals, but rations were running thin. Falik consumed more than his share of food and occupied way too much space. He'd been useless during the building process, and his single-minded focus on Halina was getting more intense by the day. Always he was glowering, moaning, plotting, planning, nursing his dream of killing her . . . even as the stench of burning flesh continued to rise from the Piaski and float in thick foul plumes across the winter sky.

The bunker proved to be less waterproof than we hoped, and regularly flooded from above and below. We didn't have a solution and hesitated to bring it up with Staszko and Kasia, whom we'd already burdened beyond measure. The best we could do was empty the rising water by hand using makeshift pails. Late at night, in total darkness, Jozek and I would form a production line: being smaller and skinnier, I'd flit back and forth through the tunnel carrying buckets of water to hand off to Jozek, who'd dump them outside as quietly as possible. It took a dozen trips or more to make a dent, and always the water would rise again after a few hours. At least it gave us something to do.

Time moved like molasses underground. There were moments when I thought I couldn't take any more of it, our bodies squeezed together in this stinking hole, eternally dark and freezing. And wet. Always wet now. But then I'd think back to Janowska . . . and consider myself lucky.

During the wee hours of November 19, 1943, while we were all taking a break in the kitchen, the dogs became agitated and started barking frantically into the distance. Trouble was on its way.

We raced back to the bunker and cowered together as a great commotion commenced outside. We heard sirens and strange dogs barking viciously. There was shouting and yelling and a commanding voice issuing orders in German. Heavy footsteps pounded directly overhead with such force that I thought for sure the bunker would cave in. Time stopped. We didn't move an inch, barely even breathed. After a seeming eternity, things quieted down.

Staszko appeared. He told us that Nazi soldiers had forced their way into the house shouting commands and questions. Staszko didn't speak German so he couldn't understand, but clearly they were searching for something. They tore through the place and all around the property, waving guns and flashlights, and left when they didn't find anything.

It was a miracle that they hadn't found us, he said. The SS canines knew we were there. They barked and sniffed incessantly in the area directly above the bunker, but their Nazi masters ignored them. Idiots. How could they not realize that the dogs had found something? More experienced officers would not have let such a thing pass. This was sheer dumb luck. Staszko was shaken to the core. Why had they come? What did they know? When would they return?

Next day, he went into town to find out what he could. A big story was on everyone's lips: the Death Brigade, the body-burning, bone-grinding band of prisoners, had staged a revolt at the Piaski. Many had escaped and fled in all directions. These were very special prisoners, eyewitnesses to key Nazi atrocities, so the SS was especially determined to hunt them down. Most of the prisoners were unfamiliar with the area and ended up running into the city, straight into the arms of their captors. Others took refuge in nearby barns and farmhouses. The luckiest ones made it into the forest. That was the safest place. The Germans, it was well known, were scared to enter there. They knew that somewhere deep in the wild dwelled Jewish and Russian resistance fighters, well hidden . . . and well armed.

We passed many hours in the bunker talking about whether it made sense to join them. But we had no idea where they were. And searching for them would be dangerous in the extreme. In spite of everything, it seemed like the wisest course of action was to simply stay where we were.

We wondered aloud sometimes what life would look like after the war, if we survived. Would there be a place for us? Where would we go? What would we do?

"Look," my father would always say at some point. "I have a brother in America. We'll go there. We'll start over again."

"And my niece and nephew," mother would add. "They're in America, too."

This image of a growing, loving family on the other side of the ocean sustained and comforted us. All we had to do was get there. All we had to do was survive.

Late one night around Christmastime, a fervent celebration for Polish Catholics when even humble farmers like Staszko and Kasia slaughtered pigs and cows for the preparation of great feasts, we were all up in the kitchen, nibbling on treats and warming ourselves by the fire, when the dogs started barking anxiously. We could hear nerves in their yips. They sensed danger. Again.

Why did trouble always seem to come when our guard was down?

I lunged for the door and everyone fell in behind

me. We scrambled into the stable, through the trapdoor, and out of sight. Jozia followed us and covered the outline of the door as best she could with loose hay. For a long time we couldn't hear anything, didn't know what was going on outside. Maybe a raid? Jozek stood near the opening, nervously clutching a butcher knife. I argued with him in hushed tones.

"You can't stab any random person who happens to open that door. You'll end up stabbing Staszko. Or Jozia. Or Michael."

He knew it was true. He looked down at the knife, thick and lethal in his hand, turned it over once or twice, then lowered it to his side. After waiting in frozen silence for what felt like days, fear thrumming our bones, Staszko descended into the bunker with hollow eyes, his mouth twitching.

"There were three of them," he said. "Men I didn't know. From the village. They stormed into the house searching for something, they wouldn't say what. I think they were hunting for Jews. Hunting for you." He looked away.

They hit Kasia, he said. "With the rifle butt. In the head. She can't see. She's blind." With that, he turned and left.

We were stunned, sickened, terrified. What would become of Kasia? And how would Staszko explain all this to the townspeople when they started asking questions? He must have let something slip on one of his drinking bouts in town. Staszko could really knock back the vodka and was a gregarious, talky drunk. We often worried about what he might be saying to whom, and overheard Kasia berate him about this many times.

"Why don't you drink at home?" she'd yell. "Then if you go mouthing off, there is no one to hear it but me!"

"Am I supposed to become a social outcast for these Jews? It's not enough that we're saving their skins?"

"The rage and guilt will eat him alive," my father said. He said little else.

A sudden snowstorm swept through and covered everything in several feet of fluffy white powder. We were relieved to hear that even more snow was on the way. Bad weather made it difficult for the Germans to advance. We knew that it would slow down the Russian forces as well, but still, a heavy blanket of white stuff provided a layer of protection. Jozia reported that everything around us had come to a standstill, except for a few trains running east, carrying ammunition and reinforcements, and a few others, operated by the Red Cross, running west, carrying wounded soldiers back to the Fatherland.

Kasia was healing, her eyesight slowly returning. My mother stole as much time as possible in the house to nurse and care for her. The frosty stillness that had descended upon our world gave us some wiggle room . . . or so we thought. Kasia's niece Stasia showed up unannounced one day and appeared in the kitchen without warning. Suddenly she was staring my mother in the face.

The dogs knew her so they hadn't barked, a constant worry of ours. Kasia had already mentioned that her brother-in-law, Stasia's father, was fiercely anti-Semitic, so we feared the worst. But Stasia turned out to be another great friend and ally, a lovely girl inside and out. Like Staszko and Kasia, Babcia, Michael, and so many others — we owed our lives to these people — she embraced us unconditionally and vowed to protect our secret. She became a regular visitor, bringing news-papers, food, and gossip from the village. A delicate, graceful young lady she was, with soft blue eyes and a tender hand. Henek took a shine to her right away. She seemed to like him too, always blushing and looking away when he paid her a compliment. Bit by bit, in the deep of winter, Stasia and Henek would fall in love.

We got lucky that time, but the scare was bracing. We resolved to keep all come-and-go to a strict minimum. But soon after, it happened again! One of Kasia's friends dropped by unexpectedly, was greeted by the dogs in silence, and caught the lot of us standing in the kitchen by the fire.

Zosia Polakova was a poor woman from a poor family who had been abused by a few men in her life. Her mother was dead, her father a drunk, and she had an illegitimate daughter.

Someone like this, uneducated and in desperate need of money, could easily be tempted to turn us in for a cash reward. Kasia implored Zosia to keep our existence a secret, but she was still recovering and we worried that she wouldn't be firm enough. Zosia literally held our lives in her hand. It was terrifying. We considered fleeing into the forest — but winter was raging and the nearest Jews were said to be twenty or thirty kilometers away. How would we reach them . . . if they were really there at all?

We talked openly to Zosia about our fears, tried to impress upon her how high the stakes were. We stressed over and over again that this was a matter of life and death, really tried to pin her down about it. She promised that no one in the world would ever hear a whisper about us from her. She had no intention of putting us in danger. We wanted to believe her, but what if she was lying? We needed another layer of protection.

Falik snapped out of his funk long enough to hatch a plan:

He would woo Zosia, make her fall in love with him, and thereby ensure our safety. We knew how persuasive he could be when he put his mind to it. His training and experience as an attorney served him well in this regard — Falik could convince anyone of anything.

It worked.

Zosia fell for him head over heels. He fawned over her whenever she was around but privately insisted that it was all an act. He felt nothing for this woman, he said. The folly was painful. We should be grateful to him for suffering through it on our behalf. My mother wasn't convinced, but I think he was telling the truth. It spooked me that he could fake emotion so credibly.

Soon he was directing Zosia to bring him small luxury items, like a proper razor and various creams and lotions — a reckless and dangerous thing to do. What would a rough-hewn peasant woman need with fancy toilette items for men? Things like that, no matter how small, were dead giveaways. Anyone would become suspicious in a minute. We warned Falik to cut it out but he shrugged us off. He was always convinced that he knew more than everybody else. Plus, he hadn't experienced Janowska, had witnessed very few horrors firsthand, and simply didn't understand just how mad and depraved the enemy was. He continued to pepper his false protestations of love with vain, indulgent requests. Zosia complied eagerly, becoming more goo-goo eyed over him by the day. I found the whole charade disturbing.

Henek and Stasia, on the other hand, were truly

in love. You could tell just by looking at them. The Nazis had murdered Henek's wife and five-year old daughter, his parents, his siblings. How do you recover from that? It's a cliché, perhaps, but nonetheless true that it begins, apparently, with love. In Stasia, Henek found a soul mate — and vice versa. A kind of lightness returned to his spirit. He seemed less depressed and his overall mood improved. He promised Stasia that he would marry her when the war was over, but what kind of promise was that? We didn't even know if we'd survive another day. I don't think I would have been able to put it into words at the time, but watching the young lovers filled me with a sense of impending heartbreak and dread. I had the same feeling, in a different way, watching Falik and Zosia. And Jozek and Jozia. They too had fallen in love.

Jozek was a strapping lad, even in these debased circumstances, and Jozia . . . how could he not fall in love with this girl? She was so fresh and pretty, such a pleasing visage to gaze upon in the midst of all this death and destruction. When she looked right at you, wow — her eyes were iridescent blue orbs, seemingly lit from within. She had a magic touch with her younger siblings, especially Romek, the baby, who always became frightened and agitated at the sight of our rawboned crew climbing up from underground. Jozia was the only one who could settle him down. She showed Jozek the same kind of care and tenderness . . . and he returned it in kind.

Everyone was pairing off. And all the pairings seemed doomed. I was happy there was no girl for me. I didn't want to go through it.

But soon Zosia offered to bring her daughter around for me. Falik was behind the idea. Again he used his lawyerly skills to argue that if I got involved with her daughter, Zosia would be even more invested in our survival. It made sense. We all agreed.

Sometimes I think he had the power to brainwash people. Maybe it was professional skill ... or maybe he was just born that way.

Dziunka Polakova

The first time I met Zosia's daughter, a shy wisp of a girl named Dziunka, Jozia hung around to help break the ice, then left us alone in the kitchen. We sat at the bare table across from each other. I knew immediately that I would not develop romantic feelings for this girl and sensed that she felt the same way. Her manner was polite and formal, proper, as if we were attending an official function — hardly the behavior of a young thing looking for love. When Zosia asked what I thought, I told the truth. But she continued to bring the girl around. Dziunka and I eventually began to relax into an easy rapport. I thought I could sense that she was opening up to the idea of romance. But I was not. And despite Falik's urging and teasing, I never tried to convince her otherwise. I was too young for that kind of trickery. Besides, I had left my heart behind in Lvov.

With Maryla Ober.

Over and over again in my mind I relived the details of our petty fight, my transfer to the day shift, her arrival at the Ghetto gates that morning after a long night of work, her transport by truck to the Piaski ... her murder. Over and over I saw bullets pound her body; watched her collapse as a pool of blood engulfed her. It was my secret torment, and I kept it to myself.

Soon, Dziunka confessed that she had a secret of her own. She was in love with an Italian Jew she met in town, a laborer. The German army maintained a few Italian and Hungarian fighting divisions in the eastern occupied territories, and these divisions routinely hired civilians, young Italian and Hungarian Jews, mostly, to dig ditches, clear roads, and do other heavy labor. Dziunka's man was one such laborer. No one knew about him, not even her mother. She begged me not to tell, and of course I didn't.

It seemed that love was everywhere that winter, true love and mock love, lost love and new love, love spawned in suffering but hopeful, ever hopeful.

Chapter Nine

~~~

Spring began to push through the snow. As the ground thawed, our bunker started flooding in earnest. The job of baling it out fell mostly to me — I had become something of an expert and was most effective when I worked alone. The floor of the bunker was constructed of poles arranged in a crisscross pattern, covered with hay. I'd push the hay aside, separate a couple of poles, use a small can to scoop out the frigid water, and dump the water into a larger bucket. When the bucket was full, I'd carry it through the tunnel and dump it outside the stable. Then I'd go back and do it again. One bucket at a time. I couldn't stop for long or I'd lose whatever progress I'd made, and the job was never really done. I didn't mind. It was a welcome distraction. We kept hearing good news about the Russian advance, but all around us the Nazis were growing more savage by the day.

The stench from the Piaski had let up somewhat during the winter months but returned with such a vengeance now that it could be incapacitating. The Death Brigade was in full force again. I held my nose, closed my eyes, tried not to breathe, tried instead to cry. Tears rarely came.

Staszko returned from the city one day with a horrifying story: He'd been drawn to a crowd gathered outside of Town Hall, pushed his way through the thick rows of people . . . and discovered a gang of brutally murdered Polish citizens on display as a bloody warning to all. Their crime? They had sheltered Jews. He told the tale in hushed tones, avoiding our gaze. We could see the exhaustion in his eyes and feared he might put us out. Who would blame him? That he and Kasia had kept us this long was remarkable.

His trips into the city became less frequent after that, but by some miracle he never spoke of sending us away. I don't know what he was thinking. I'm not sure I would have had the faith and courage to make the same choice had our roles been reversed. Some part of me was convinced that the whole lot of us would soon be discovered and killed. I could see the scene play out in grisly detail in my mind, prayed it was not a premonition.

As if to confirm my worst fears, Staszko came thrashing into the bunker one April morning in a fierce panic. Two German trucks and a couple of cars were headed in our direction. There were no roads for them to take, they were plowing right through the fields, straight toward us, so close that there wasn't even time to flee into the forest! Staszko hastily sealed the entrance to the bunker and rushed away.

We waited in silence for our executioners, confident that they would murder us on the spot along with the entire Niedziolka family. If we were lucky they might ship us to Janowska first. That was our best hope. I don't remember what I was thinking or feeling in those moments. I must have been in a kind of shock state. It went on like that for a long time. Too long. Hours, even. We listened hard, heard nothing. Henek buried his remaining gold pieces in the soft ground.

"At least they won't go to the Reich," he said.

Finally, late in the day, there was a rustling at the door. Our bodies tensed . . . but we knew from the sound of his touch that it was Staszko. He slipped inside wearing a feeble smile. The Nazis were still here, just above our heads. But they had not come for us.

Several officers of the Gestapo had decided that this was a perfect spot for an equestrian event. Who knows how or why? They'd brought in fine horses and tons of equipment and set it all up on a plot of land directly adjacent to the bunker. We were dumbfounded. This made no sense even by simple logic, since the site they chose was soft and wet, practically a swamp. The whole thing was ludicrous. Curiosity overwhelmed me and I asked Staszko if I could take a peek from the attic. He said yes, and before my mother could snatch me back I slipped out of the bunker, into the stable, and up into the attic to peer through the familiar cracks in the roof tiles. The scene outside was surreal.

High-ranking Gestapo officers, perhaps even a few generals, joined by elegant ladies in fine clothing, lounged on lawn chairs, their horses lolling nearby, surrounded by tables groaning with food and wine, eating lunch off of fine china. I watched in disbelief for a while, then fled back down into the bunker.

My mother's eyes went wide as eggs when I described the scene. My father was the first to laugh. Once he started, we all collapsed in hushed guffaws. It was too ridiculous, Nazis cavorting with horses in a swamp above our heads, Jews hiding literally beneath their feet. Could they feel the rumble of our laughter in their boots? They came back a few more times after that, always the same routine — horses, banquet tables, pretty ladies — and then stopped coming. The whole episode lives in my memory like a crazy dream.

Good news continued to trickle in as Russian

forces made steady progress against the Germans. And then, on April 15, 1944, a big break:

The Red Army took control of Tarnopol, just sixty kilometers east of Lvov. So close! We would be next! This beleaguered town on the Russian border had been seized by and won back from the Germans multiple times since the start of the war in bloody battles in which thousands were killed, but the German army had been decimated by the rough winter and it looked like the Russians would hold Tarnopol for good this time. Misko wept when he told us.

"Get ready to live again," he said. "You're going to be free people soon."

We allowed ourselves to believe it. Babcia even cooked a feast and served it to us in the bunker — roast beef and golabki with all the trimmings — in celebration, she said, of our coming liberation. Liberation. I thought of it as a physical thing, something I could grab with my hand. I imagined naively that my old life might still be waiting for me out there, that I might be able to slip back into it as I would an old pair of trousers.

Our optimism was premature. Indeed, it seemed that every time we allowed ourselves a glimmer of hope, the tide turned against us. We learned that the Russians would pause in Tarnopol to regroup and restock supply lines before pushing west toward Lvov. This would take a few weeks or more, so we'd have to wait at least that long before they would reach us.

Then Staszko came with worse news yet: Two high-ranking Wehrmacht officers had come to the house and announced that the Niedziolka family had four days to evacuate. They were to take whatever they could carry and get out. Their property was expected to become a battle zone, and the army was seizing it.

"So that's it," Staszko said. "It's over."

And just like that, our world went upside down. Again.

Hasty evacuation plans were made. Staszko, Kasia and the kids would stay in Babcia's house until they could figure out a better solution. It would be a tight fit but they'd manage. Henek and Falik would hide in Zosia's place, a dangerous bet with neighbors so close by but better than nothing. Mother, father, Jozek and I tried not to panic. What about us?

We knew our parents couldn't bring themselves to do it, so Jozek and I asked Babcia if we could stay with her for a short time. We promised that Jozek and I would leave after a couple of days, steal into our old neighborhood to find a safe place, then send for our parents to join us. A dangerous scheme to be sure, but what were the options? Babcia agreed. We knew she would.

Babcia. I've held her in my heart every day of my life for seventy years and more.

But how would we get from Staszko's farm to Babcia's house undetected? Michael arrived with his big horse-drawn wagon loaded with straw. He hid my parents inside the load and drove them to Babcia's house, then came back to transport Jozek and me the same way. Up in the driver's seat, he smiled and whistled like it was just some ordinary day — born actor, brilliant soul.

The room Babcia made for us was tiny and windowless, like a closet. We slept not a wink, jumped at every sound, and desperately searched for a better solution. On the second day, as promised, Jozek and I prepared to set off. It would not be easy to get out of the neighborhood — we couldn't cut across the forest because the SS was stationed there, at the Piaski, and we'd need to cross three sets of heavily guarded railroad tracks in order to reach it. We decided instead to take the old country road. We kissed our parents goodbye and slipped away through the back of the house.

We had to attempt the trip during daylight hours since we couldn't walk through populated areas after curfew. We made our way to the edge of town as inconspicuously as possible, but hadn't gotten more than half a mile away when we ran into my old pal Dziunka, Zosia's daughter, walking with a couple other girls. She cocked her head strangely at us but knew not to say a word. Her friends glanced at us sidelong, suspicious. We decided it was too risky to continue on this way, reversed course, and doubled back to a nearby cemetery where we figured we could hide out until nightfall. We appeared to be the only living souls around. Jozek spotted a small wooden shack in the distance — a trupiarnia, or mortuary — and we headed toward it. It was a tiny room, hot and humid, with high ceilings and a small loft up top. Jozek climbed on my back to hoist himself up there, then reached down and pulled me up by my arms. We spent half the day lying quietly in the loft, anxiously waiting for sunset. The skies opened up and a torrential rain began to pound the shack. Then, through a crack in the wall, we saw a very strange sight:

A young couple appeared out of nowhere, running through the rain, and were heading right for the shack! Jozek and I held our breath as they entered. We tried not to make a sound. If we could wait this out in silence they might leave and not discover us. The rain continued. I grew restless. I shifted my weight and some dust and lime from the rafters drifted down upon the couple. The young woman got spooked.

"What if there are devils up there?"

Her boyfriend laughed, lifted her up, dared her to take a look. Suddenly the poor girl found herself nose-to-nose with a pair of filthy, emaciated apparitions. She screamed her head off.

"Devils!" she cried shrilly. "Devils!"

Her boyfriend wasn't laughing now. The two of them ran away in a panic. But Jozek had already recognized the boy as an old friend. We jumped down and ran after them.

"Kazik!" Jozek called.

Kazik turned around . . . and a warm wave of recognition flooded his face. He laughed and walked back over to us, embraced us. His girlfriend smiled and blushed, apologized for alarming us. We didn't need to explain our situation; it was obvious. These gentle young souls asked how they could help. They offered to bring coffee, bread, cigarettes, even money. I could hardly believe our luck. We arranged to meet them again later that day with the promised supplies.

As we waited for them to return, nervousness set in. Stories like this often ended badly — it was not uncommon for people to behave as Kazik and his girlfriend had, only to return with the Gestapo or SS. Was this a trick? Would they trade us in for cash? We decided to hide a good distance away so we would see who they came back with. If they had indeed betrayed us, we might still have a chance to escape.

But hours later, as promised, Kazik and the girl appeared, alone, bearing food and supplies. Relief came over us in waves. They loaded us up with coffee, sandwiches, cigarettes and cash, and the four of us had a nice picnic among the dead.

Their kindness and generosity that day shifted something inside me. For a moment, earlier, while we were still waiting, I had convinced myself that they would betray us. I couldn't stop the feeling from filling my gut and heart. But now, in the damp lazy quiet, with goodness flowing from their eyes and by their hand, I was reminded that miracles like this were still possible. People like this existed. Good still prevailed sometimes. And luck. There was that, too. There was goodness and luck.

When it was time to say goodbye, I kissed Kazik and his girlfriend tenderly on their cheeks, kisses that linger still.

It was dark now, after curfew. Jozek and I decided to make our way back to our old neighborhood by cutting through backyards and gardens, moving stealthily, cat-like. As we passed through a large plot of vegetables, we spotted two Ukrainian soldiers with machine guns walking down the center of the very railroad tracks we needed to cross. We dropped to the ground, kept our heads low, waited for them to pass. Had they seen us? I didn't think so . . . but they could be sneaking up on us right now.

My brother took a peek. The soldiers were walking away. We waited until they faded into the distance and then tore off, putting as much distance between them and us as possible. Eventually, we had to cross the tracks. We knew that soldiers hid in many of the bushy areas along the way, waiting to ambush people like us. But crossing out in the open was just as dangerous. We decided upon the latter, figuring we'd at least avoid a direct ambush. Even if someone saw us, maybe we could run fast enough to get away.

We got across the tracks safely and sprinted from there into the old neighborhood. What we saw shocked and terrified us. Most of the buildings and landmarks of our youth had been bombed and burned to rubble. Our beloved synagogue was being used as a horse stable and truck garage. The site was empty where my grandparents' house once stood. It was dizzying to encounter only ruins and ash at all the landmark places of my youth. The remaining streets and houses were filled with strangers — even most of our Gentile neighbors were gone. I'm not sure what I expected, but this was worse.

We walked over to the home of the Kostaszcuks, a good Polish Catholic family we'd known for many years. Jozek and I had played with the two Kostaszcuk boys in the local soccer club, and Mrs. Kostaszcuk was known to hand out chocolate soda and fruit from her garden to the neighborhood kids. I was filled with hope when she answered the door. We asked if she'd be willing to hide the four of us on her property — my parents, Jozek, and me — until the Russians came. The Red Army was firmly on the march again so it wouldn't be long now, maybe a week or two. Mrs. K's eyes filled with tears. She looked away. The area was crowded, she said. The Piaski was nearby. Her neighbors were war-weary and unpredictable. It was all too dangerous, we'd be discovered in no time. We knew she was right.

We tried a few other remaining neighbors but everyone felt the same way. No one would take the risk. I couldn't blame them.

Our last hope was Polku Silvester, an old friend of Jozek's. I waited out back while Jozek went inside. After a few minutes, he returned with a grim-faced companion. Polku gestured for us to follow him to a spot from which we could get a full view of the neighborhood without being seen.

"Take a look," he said. "You're crazy to be here. The Germans have everything sealed up now that the Russians are so close. Soldiers everywhere. You even see them sleeping outdoors, right in the open, because there's no place else to put them." The scene before our eyes confirmed it.

We were less afraid of the Wehrmacht forces than the SS, but there were plenty of Jew-haters among them. And Polku said their presence was stoking the flames of local anti-Semitism. People were open in their hatred for Jews as never before. The place was toxic. We said goodbye and headed back the way we came. What now?

There was nowhere to go but back to Babcia's. After that, we'd have to retreat into the forest. We'd first heard about the forest dwellers, fighters and resistors, back when we worked at the Schwarz factory, but no one had ever been able to confirm their existence. A man named Zisel had tried to find and join them but returned a week later empty-handed. Zisel would never say that there was no one out there, only that he couldn't find them. I understood the choice. As long as there was a chance they existed, we could hope to join them if things ever came to that. Staszko used to mention the forest dwellers once in a while, and seemed to know a lot about them — they were twenty or thirty kilometers to the east, well armed and well organized. We were never sure how he knew all this and sometimes wondered if he was saying it as an enticement for us to leave. The existence of an armed resistance was to us more an article of faith than a proven fact, but it was looking more and more like our best hope.

Jozek and I retraced our steps from the day: over railroad tracks, through yards and gardens, fields and alleyways, all the way back to the cemetery. We decided to spend the night there. It was after midnight. We found a good spot and settled down. My heart was sinking fast. I didn't see how we would make it through these last few weeks. Then my eyes fell on the mausoleum we had been in earlier, and others like it scattered about. Why not stay here? We could pilfer food from local gardens, and Babcia could set us up with some staple items to last a while. Jozek and I agreed that it might work for the two of us . . . but it would be far more dangerous for a family of four. And the thought of leaving my parents behind was unbearable.

No. The forest. It would have to be the forest.

Exhausted, I put my head down among the tombstones and tried to sleep. After a moment, I jumped back up. Jozek gave me a look.

"You're going to laugh," I said, "but I know it's true. The Russian offensive starts now. I can hear it!"

And I could — a steady rumble from not too far away, echoing underground, softly rattling the bones of the dead.

"Don't be stupid," said Jozek.

"Put your ear to the ground," I insisted. Listen."

He did, but remained skeptical. I knew I was right.

By the time we got back to Babcia's house, my father had heard it too. The next day, Staszko came to us with a great smile and confirmed it.

"You go nowhere," he said. "You stay right here."

Soon planes roared overhead, bombs exploded in the distance. The Germans ran west in a panic, blowing up everything in their path in an effort to destroy evidence and demolish any potential spoils of war. How long would it take for the Russian army to secure Babcia's village? A day or two? Longer? A week? We didn't know if we'd survive this last stretch, with Katyusha rockets blasting overhead, smashing and burning the rubble-strewn landscape.

But one day toward the end of July 1944, a Russian patrol appeared on the main road. Another patrol appeared behind it, at a distance of about fifty feet. Then others. The next day even more Russians came around, and finally it was safe for us to step outside.

Safe. Just like that.

Chapter Ten

$\sim\!\sim\!\sim$

We headed out of Babcia's house in the early morning and walked in the direction of home. It was strange to be out in the open as a family like this. We hadn't gotten very far when we were stopped by a group of Russian soldiers who commanded us to take cover. The Germans were just a couple of blocks away, they said, shooting in our direction. We had no choice but to retreat for a few days — we hadn't lived through this hellish odyssey only to get killed now. The Russians put us up in strange houses, some occupied, some empty, and gave us good food to eat while we waited out the fighting. They promised to protect us and come back in the event of an emergency.

"We won't let the Fritzes catch you," they said.

And they didn't.

Within a week or so, the entire length of the main street was lined with Russian tanks. Other streets and roads were teeming with trucks, motorcades, and foot soldiers. The Red Army was on the march! How far to Berlin?

We ran into a young Jewish woman we'd known since forever, a sweet soul named Cyla Brandwein. I was surprised and thrilled to learn that she and her husband Nat were still alive. The last time I'd seen Cyla was more than a year earlier, in April 1943, a day or two after the Schwarz factory murders. I had stayed home from work that day so I could search for my cousin — she was on the night shift but I'd heard a rumor that she might have escaped.

I went to her house, went to nearby hiding places, asked around . . . but could feel in my heart that I would not find her, that she had been murdered along with the rest. She was wherever they were now. I remember questioning as I trudged along with leaden feet why we should continue to struggle for survival. What was it for? My sister was dead. My girlfriend, dead. Best friends, cousins, aunts and uncles, neighbors, shop owners, school chums, teammates from my soccer days — all dead. Surely we were next. Why go on? What was the point? As these thoughts shrouded my mind and spirit, I turned down Weisenhofer Street and walked past a large private house that had been converted into a Jewish police station — three stories tall, with big picture windows at street level. I heard a frantic tapping on the glass and turned toward it.

It was Cyla Brandwein, on the other side of the window, trapped inside.

She had been rounded up with dozens of other Jews and was about to be "processed" and shipped off to Janowska Concentration Camp. She screamed when she saw me, begged me to come inside and get her out. I walked in and looked around — it was sometimes

Cyla Brandwein

possible to extract a favor from a Jewish policeman you knew from the neighborhood — but recognized no one in authority. When I went back outside and told Cyla the bad news through the window, she cried and urged me to fetch her brother-in-law, Mayr. Luckily he was home when I got to his place, said he knew someone in charge, and raced away to try to save Cyla's life. I never saw her again after that. I guess I had always assumed the worst.

But now here she was, safe and sound.

Cyla and I would revisit that day on Weisenhofer Street many times over the coming days, months, and years. What if I had not happened by at that moment? What if her brother had not been home? What would have become of her? She would never have been reunited with her husband, never have children and raise a family. Was it all a matter of luck? Is that, in the end, what our survival came down to? It was a miracle that we survived, a series of fantastically lucky breaks and near misses, starting, for Jozek and me, with that cheerful young driver who helped us break out of Janowska. Bless him. Had he been caught, he would have been tortured and killed.

And Grzesko. He put his life on the line by leading my parents out of the city to their hiding place. It is a one hundred percent certainty that all three of them would have been executed if caught. The same was true of Stasko, Kasia, and the Niedziolka children; and Babcia, Michael, Stasia, Misko, Zosia — all of us. But we had survived.

How was it possible? And why? By what miracle and for what purpose had our lives been spared? A common call among our suffering people was, "If you survive, tell the world what happened here." I suppose that is purpose enough.

Cyla told us that she and Nat spent the war years hiding in the attic of their neighbor's house, a kind Polish lady named Mrs. Gromadowska. Nat was still there. She had ventured out only to check on the situation. Mrs. Gromadowska and her family had treated them extremely well, but at one point the situation got too hot and Mrs. G tearfully asked them to leave. A neighbor, it seems, had become suspicious, and Mrs. G feared that her house would soon be raided. Cyla and Nat begged her to reconsider, and the woman promised to consult her priest about it. A short time later she returned and asked their forgiveness.

The priest, she said, wouldn't hear of putting them out. "G-d forbid you make them leave," he said. "Keep these Jewish people close to you, save their lives, and Jesus will take care of the rest."

Simple human decency and kindness will prevail over monstrous evil wherever there is enough will and courage to make it so. We lived this simple truth over and over again. It made us weep right there on the street, as Cyla told her tale.

Just then, a Russian solider ran toward us and yelled at the top of his lungs, "The Germans are coming! Get over! Get over!" He gestured wildly at a six-foot tall fence. We knew my mother couldn't climb it, so Lonek, a young Jewish man I didn't know very well, grabbed her by the shoulders as I grabbed her by the feet. With the help of a Russian soldier, we got her over the top. We did the same thing with Cyla. We all took cover wherever we could while the Russians brought in more patrols and beat the Germans back.

When it was over, we continued on to the old neighborhood. It was even more decimated than before, barely recognizable. We'd learn in the coming days that the SS had slaughtered many of our Christian neighbors for hiding or helping Jews. Others had been shipped off to forced labor camps in Germany. Some volunteered to work for the military in Germany. And some ran away, disappeared. They were the ones who had cooperated with the Nazis. They knew what to expect in return for their betrayal. I don't think there was a single survivor at that moment incapable of tearing such a traitor apart with his or her bare hands.

The pain of looking out onto rubble-strewn lots that once teemed with the people and places of my life was something I experienced bodily — a gnawing ache in my head and belly. But you go on. You have no choice.

Cyla and Nat made the happy discovery that their house was still intact — a nice big place with plenty of rooms on a good amount of property. They insisted that we stay with them. Nat had owned and operated a successful bakery business before the war, along with his mother and five brothers, none of whom, apparently, had survived. (His father had died of cancer in 1937, a couple of years before the War started.)

No sooner had we moved into the Brandwein house than other old friends and neighbors began straggling in, refugees from our former existence, some to stay, others just to visit, all bearing food and news and stories.

So this was liberation. We had crawled out from the bunker naked and penniless, stripped of any vestige of our former existence, and now wandered numbly through haunted, smoking ruins. I was no longer an over-indulged child. I was . . . what? I didn't know, didn't recognize myself. My eyes had seen killing on an incomprehensible scale, children murdered by the score. My lungs had ingested the incinerated flesh of hundreds of thousands of victims. They were part of me now. What did that make me? Who was I? Who were we as a family? How would we ever again live normal lives?

We trekked out to the piece of land we owned, where my father kept the stables, and discovered only wreckage. No matter. What we'd come for was buried underground. We cleared a certain spot and prepared to dig when a couple of Catholic neighbors walked over.

"It's gone," they said. "The SS found it and took it away."

No. No, no, no!

Boxes of gold and silver, a small fortune in buried treasure worth a thousand times its real value in this desperate moment . . . gone. Dora and Morris Panzer, my mother's sister and her husband, had entrusted the cache to us a couple of years earlier, before fleeing to Warsaw, and asked my father to bury it on his property. There were gems, too, lots of them — diamonds, rubies, emeralds, sapphires — but my aunt had refused to part with these. I remember standing in her sunny kitchen as she showed me a well-worn apron into the seams of which she had sewn the precious stones. She stuffed the apron into a slop closet, among the rags. Who would think to look there?

"Better they end up in the dump," she said, "than in Nazi hands."

Uncle Morris and Aunt Dora's mom-and-pop jewelry business, which they started in their apartment, was so successful that they eventually opened a big elegant shop in the Rynek, Lvov's central square. They moved into a sprawling apartment at 4 Boimów Street, an excellent address, and led what seemed to me a glamorous, worldly existence. My cousins Zygmunt and Paula, their children, about the same ages as Jozek and Clara, were well educated and highly polished. Zygmunt lived in Paris, and was studying to become an engineer. Paula, who we called Pepa, was married to a fine young doctor. These were our fancy relatives . . . but so loving and generous. They threw the greatest parties. The best birthday and holiday gifts always came from Aunt Dora and Uncle Morris. They were forever showering us with rare treats like chocolate oranges from Italy or luscious French bon-bon.

Morris was a good all-around craftsman and built four solid boxes of lustrous dark wood, expertly joined, to contain the gold and silver. The boxes, which looked to me like child-size coffins, were filled with precious metals, sealed, and transported to the stables in the deep of night. They had to be buried cleverly and quickly — it was imperative that we not get caught in the act. A spot inside one of the stables was chosen, right where the horses used to eat (they were gone by then), and Jozek managed to dig a sizable ditch in under an hour. We lowered the boxes into the ground, backfilled the hole, and piled some wood on top as camouflage. No one would guess there was anything under there.

Zygmund was drafted to serve as an engineer for the Russian Army soon after we buried the treasure (he had dropped his studies and returned to Lvov right after the Russian occupation). Paula and her husband used their connections to get good Christian documents, fled to Warsaw as Polish Catholics, and disappeared into a city of strangers. Aunt Dora, according to plan, disguised herself as a Christian, secured the proper documents, and joined them in Warsaw. Next it was

Morris's turn.

This particular deception was harder for men to pull off — if the Gestapo ordered you to drop your pants, as they often did, it was all over. Jews posing as Christians were special targets, frequently exposed by "friends," neighbors, and paid spies. The Gestapo had a tight grip on the rail system, so Morris couldn't risk traveling by train.

It was safest to go by car. My father's good friend, a professional driver who knew all the ins and outs of the road, agreed to help. He dressed Morris in a dirty verszalung, or cover-all, got him the necessary identification card, loaded him onto the back of the truck as a worker, and drove him all the way to Warsaw. They passed the checkpoints with flying colors, and soon Morris was reunited with his family.

The Panzers lived together in safety for a while. But then someone smelled a rat. The Gestapo stormed their apartment one night and dragged them away to be killed.

Now here we stood, empty-handed in the rubble, where once their treasure had lain. (Zygmund ended up serving in the Russian Army for the remainder of the war, and then moved to Israel, where he lived until his death.)

How did the Nazis know the treasure was there? Someone must have tipped them off. But who? Only our immediate family knew of its whereabouts. My parents wracked their brains over the mystery. Jozek and I knew the answer but breathed not a word. It was better left unsolved. The truth would be harder for my parents to bear:

After losing our money in a card game, Jozek had become obsessed with trying to earn it back. In a panicky move, he mentioned the buried treasure to a young Ukrainian policeman he knew and liked. They struck a deal to retrieve the loot, sell it on the black market, and split the earnings. But when they drove out to the stables they found the entire area crawling with soldiers.

The Germans had just been defeated at Stalingrad and were streaming back across Poland. There was no choice but to retreat and try some other time. That time never came ... for Jozek, anyway. This was probably a blessing. It was nearly impossible to sell such valuable items on the black market in those days — no one had enough cash to pay for them — and the Ukrainian policeman would likely have killed Jozek and stolen the stash before they could even try.

Out and about in Lvov, 1944, just after liberation

Jozek had confessed the whole sordid affair to me sometime after our escape from Janowska, but somehow we both continued to believe that the treasure remained hidden safely underground, just waiting for us to dig it up one day. Magical thinking, I guess. We did a lot of that.

Chapter Eleven

~~~

I was standing outside the Brandwein house one day, watching in fascination as a line of Russian T-34 tanks rolled by, when a Studebaker truck pulled up and parked at the curb. A man jumped out, helped an old woman climb down, and the two of them started walking toward the front door. As they got closer I recognized them: Nat's brother Lester and old Mrs. Brandwein, their mother. They had survived after all.

Lester told us over schnapps and brisket that he had posed as a Catholic, secured working papers, and landed a job running a large German folwark, an industrial agricultural plantation, out in the countryside. He placed his mother, who pretended to be deaf and dumb, in the care of nearby farmers, paid the humble folk to look after her, and visited whenever he could. Miraculously, it had all worked out.

That's how it was in those early days of liberation — people materialized out of thin air, apparition-like, each with a new twist on the same tale.

A survivor's registry was established in Lvov, and I volunteered to go add the names of my family and the Brandweins. Scrolling eagerly though the pages, I discovered that my first cousin Wisia Werner had survived, along with her husband Artur and their two young children. I'd later learn that they'd posed as Polish Catholics, even going so far as to have their son become an altar boy in the local church. (The whole family eventually moved to Israel.)

It was a great relief to see their names in the book

...but I could find no others. I searched and searched. There had to be someone. I had dozens of friends and neighbors and a huge family before the war. Had none survived? Not one? How was it possible? Others around me, also poring through the lists of names, were making the same discovery.

The decimation of our people was near total. That any of us remained at all seemed like a miracle. I learned to be deeply grateful for every new survivor who showed up at the Brandwein house.

Manny Grosberg walked through the front door one day like it was the most natural thing in the world. Manny! Before the war he'd been in charge of running a special division of the Brandwein bakery business dedicated solely to the production of Passover matzo. He was by all accounts a loyal, hard-working employee and friend, beloved for his natural charisma and raucous sense of humor. What a joy to see him alive! We asked how he managed to survive and he just shook his head from side to side as it to say, "You wouldn't believe it." And we almost didn't.

His whole family had been murdered (I am numb with having to repeat those words over and over again) and he knew he was next. He moved away to an area where nobody knew him. Manny didn't look Jewish at all so he figured he'd have a decent chance of passing as Polish Catholic. Except that you could hear his Yiddish accent from a block away. There was no time to work on losing it, so he came up with an ingenious solution: He'd fake a stutter. It would be much harder to detect his accent that way. He practiced and practiced until he had it down pat. Worked like a charm. The stutter not only masked his heavy Yiddish inflections but inspired strangers to treat him with extra care and consideration, as if he were feeble-minded or seriously disabled. I was amused and delighted by this clever ruse and asked Manny to give us a sample right there around the table.

"Sure!" he said, always game to put on a show, and spoke a few sentences with a profound stutter. Completely convincing. No hint that it wasn't authentic.

We laughed our heads off. This was a new one. Manny might be the only Jew in Poland who'd managed to survive this way. I guffawed down to my belly for the first time in years.

We heard that there were other survivors from the neighborhood still in hiding in the forest, afraid to venture out. An armed gang of young Ukrainian men fighting for an independent Ukraine, the Banderowcy, were also hiding in the forest, closer to the periphery, and opened fire randomly on any Russian vehicle within range. Many innocent people were killed this way, and Jews hiding deeper in the forest rightfully feared getting caught in the crossfire on their way out.

But eventually they started to trickle back. The first stop for everyone was the Brandwein house. Here you could get food and shelter, news and comfort, connect with others, take stock, make a plan. The Russian army commissioned the Brandweins to bake bread for the troops, and everyone chipped in their labor. The Brandwein house became well known during the summer and fall of 1944 as "the Jewish house" . . . and deserves to be remembered that way by history.

What had become of my old friend Bronek? I asked everyone about him. When finally I learned his fate, I wished I never had:

It was unusually cold for the month of April when

he first went into hiding in the old neighborhood — spring seemed reluctant to settle in that fetid place and time — but Bronek managed to shelter and feed himself undetected . . . for a while. Then someone ratted him out to the SS. They didn't even bother to arrest him, just sent a bunch of goons from the Piaski to beat him in the street so brutally that spectators tried to stop it, a rare thing. They kicked and stomped his face and chest into the concrete until he was dead. I heard the story over and over. There were scores of witnesses.

Bronek.

My best friend. Son of my father's best friend. I knew him as a sunny, hopeful guy, a carefree spirit with a ready smile. And that's how I shall always remember him.

Many of the people who helped and supported us in the Jewish house were our righteous Gentile neighbors, the same ones, most of them, who had sheltered Jewish friends and neighbors during the war. In my experience during three years of Nazi occupation, I found that the kindest and most helpful Polish and Ukrainian Catholics were the poorest among them. The more humble their circumstance, the more generous they seemed to be. Let it be recorded and remembered: In that time and place, humble folk saved Jewish lives in droves.

One such woman, a Polish Catholic, I forget her name, mentioned in passing that Dora Schrank had survived and was living in her family's house alone, praying for her father's return. Dora was at that very moment sitting with a neighbor — the very same neighbor who had saved the girl's life in the first place by hiding her in some garden bushes when the SS raided her house and dragged her mother away.

Dora Schrank. It seemed like a lifetime ago that her father Nathan and I had huddled and whispered in some dank corner of the Janowska Camp, I offering him a chance to escape with us, he waiting to secure a hiding place close to his daughter. Now she was sitting at a kitchen table just down the block. I raced over there in a flash. Dora, about fourteen years old at the time though she looked younger, was barely recognizable — two heads taller than when I'd last seen her, and thin like a toothpick. She asked right away about her father. I told her about the last time I'd seen him. All we could do was wait, see if he showed up. Her mother, she knew, was dead. Dora was an only child — her mother had had a difficult pregnancy and was unable to give birth again — so she was truly alone in the world. We talked and talked that day and in the days that followed, and over the course of time Dora's story came out.

The tale of Dora Schrank, also known as Theresa Ackerman, is a fascinating one, and I recount it here to the best of my ability:

Back when we were still living in the open Ghetto, going in and out only for work, Nathan Shrank was assigned to a small detail doing odd jobs in Lvov — sawing wood, cleaning trucks, clearing roads, and so on. The head overseer of this team of workers was a young Polish-speaking German officer named Ackerman, from Schlesien, near the Polish border. He knew and loved the Polish language and took a shine to Nathan right away. The two men struck up an unlikely friendship. The officer and his wife wanted to help Nathan and Dora. His own sister had died in Germany when she was around Dora's age, so he felt especially protective of the young girl.

It was not completely uncommon to find German officers who disproved of Hitler's regime and took quiet measures to help Jews and other victims, but what this man offered to do was extraordinary: he would travel back to Germany, get his sister's birth certificate, give it to Dora, and take her into his home using his dead sister's identity. He and his wife lived in Grodek Jagiellónski, some distance away from Lvov, so it was unlikely that anyone would recognize the girl. The plan was perfect, and Nathan gratefully leapt at the opportunity. But when he explained it all to Dora, she absolutely refused to go.

"You must do this," Nathan said. "These are good people. They'll keep you safe. You'll be a nice German girl now. Theresa Ackerman. Isn't that a pretty name?"

Dora wailed and wailed, desperate not to be separated from her father, but eventually relented and moved away to become Theresa Ackerman. She was a city girl who knew nothing about farm life, living suddenly on a great estate with cows, horses, pigs and all kinds of other animals. Officer Ackerman's mother-in-law, who also lived on the estate, tucked Dora under her wing.

Grandma, as Dora called her, started taking Theresa to church, and even introduced her to the priest — I guess as her son-in-law's sister, but I can't be certain. On their frequent walks to and from services, Dora would see emaciated prisoners from a nearby concentration camp doing roadwork and other labor, and started carrying bits of bread to toss at them as she went by. A young girl might be able to get away with this behavior but any adult approval of it would mean big trouble. Grandma publicly scolded Dora, as she knew she must, and privately warned the girl to be more careful. Theresa promised not to take any more chances . . . but Dora, apparently, had other ideas.

She slipped away one morning, desperate to see her father, and hopped a train to Lvov. From there, she jumped on a trolley car that would take her out near the Ghetto. She noticed another passenger looking at her funny and recognized him as a neighborhood boy, a kid from a decent family, the Schneiders. His gaze made her nervous so she jumped off at the next stop. But this rotten kid jumped out after her and exposed her as a Jew to a Ukrainian policeman. She was arrested and dragged to the Sobieskiego School, headquarters of the Ukrainian police force. There she was interrogated roughly but stuck to her story: She was German, the younger sister of a ranking officer. Policemen were dispatched to Grodek Jagiellónski to investigate. Soon Officer Ackerman came thundering through the front doors, demanding Theresa's release.

"Ukrainian pigs!" he shouted. "How dare you arrest my sister, a good German girl! I'll have your heads for this!"

He played it for all it was worth, insulting and intimidating everyone in sight and demanding an apology. He could pull rank like this with the Ukrainians. Had Dora been in the custody of the SS it would have been a very different story. The police released Ackerman's "sister" at once, and promised it would never happen again.

That night, Ackerman gave Dora a serious talking-to. She must never pull anything like that again. She could have gotten them all killed. Soon after that Dora learned that the Ghetto had been liquidated . . . and her father, shipped to Janowska.

The Ackerman house was often filled with German

friends and relations of the officer and his wife, all of whom, Dora said, hated and cursed Hitler and couldn't wait for the end of war. They knew that the Nazis would soon be defeated and were anxious to return to their homes and families in the Fatherland. Still, their presence unnerved her and she always managed to find some outdoor task or activity that would keep her well out of sight.

Her "brother" continued to show Dora nothing but kindness and generosity, even in the face of her occasionally erratic behavior, and frequently invited her to sneak with him into the cellar to listen to news bulletins on a contraband radio. Dora heard Stalin's speech to the world this way, crouching among garden tools and canned fruits and vegetables, heartened by the promise that Russia would soon rid Poland of the Nazi scourge. Radio Free Europe was strictly verboten. Even owning a radio could result in death, especially for a German officer.

As the Russian advance intensified and liberation grew near, Germans started fleeing back to their homeland in droves. Officer Ackerman and his family stayed in Grodek Jagielloński as long as they could. When they had to leave, they begged Theresa to join them. But she wanted to stay. She wanted to be liberated and reunited with her father. The Ackermans had no choice but to leave her behind.

She squatted in their house alone for a brief time, but fled when the fighting came too close. The house was soon demolished. Dora wandered the countryside, homeless and desperate, foraging and seeking shelter where she could.

Eventually, she came upon a little shack in which lived a dirt-poor family of eight — mother, father, and six young children. They agreed to put Dora up for a while and she was grateful. But soon she was living in terror. The man of the house was a vicious drunk who beat his wife daily. There was never any food around and the kids were always hungry and crying.

One day, Dora managed to gather some provisions — the tenacious girl had crawled low along nearby fields to collect potatoes and other root vegetables — and cooked a big meal. The drunken man didn't like it and threw the whole platter up against the ceiling.

Dora tried again a few days later, crawling through the fields to claw out what she could, when major fighting erupted around her and she was nearly killed.

The Russians had arrived.

It didn't take them long to seize Grodek Jagielloński. Suddenly it was safe to leave. Dora thanked the family, hit the road, and hitchhiked back to Lvov.

And now here she was, living alone in an empty house, waiting for her father to appear. I knew he'd probably been killed at Janowska and I think she knew it too, but we never spoke those words aloud to each other.

The Schrank house, built in 1938, was a spacious, modern affair, intended as the new headquarters of the family's thriving retail and wholesale grocery business. It had several outbuildings and other structures specially designed for storing corn, wheat and other perishables, some of which were equipped with refrigeration — a sophisticated operation by local standards. The thought of Dora rattling around alone in that big empty place broke my heart, and I urged her to come stay with us at the Brandweins. Her answer was always the same.

"I'm waiting for my father."

Days passed. No Nathan. What would she do?

She announced one day that a kindly Russian family had offered to adopt her. These remarkable people had always been good to the Schranks. The man of the house, director of a yeast factory, had offered to take the whole family along when war broke out in 1941 and he and his family were required to return to Russia. But like so many other Jews, Nathan and his wife elected to stay, never believing that the Germans would go as far as they did.

Now that conditions in Lvov were secure again, the family had returned to reopen the factory and get back to work. They were shattered to learn that Nathan and his wife had not survived, and immediately gave Dora a job looking after children in a day care center within the factory building — they were progressive thinkers and strove to create a collegial, communal workplace atmosphere. They invited Dora live with them, and offered to adopt her.

"But I want to go to Palestine," she said. Her heart was newly set on living in the Holy Land. Many surviving Jews were planning to immigrate there, and there were several relocation programs designed especially for children who'd been orphaned by the war. We tried to persuade Dora to stay with us, but her mind was made up.

Chapter Twelve

~~~

In February 1945, seven months after our liberation, and seven months before the war actually ended, the Yalta Conference convened the "Big Three" world leaders — FDR, Churchill, and Stalin — to discuss terms for reestablishing the nations of war-torn Europe. As a result of conference negotiations, Russia would be permitted to keep the territory of eastern Poland it had annexed in 1939. In return, Poland would be allowed to expand its western borders into German territory, and Polish citizens living in the Russian-occupied zones would be allowed to register for the right to resettle in western Poland.

We wanted to get out of Eastern Europe, and planned to register for resettlement as soon as the rolls were open. Meanwhile, the Soviets were still drafting young Jewish and Ukrainian men into the army . . . and Jozek and I both received cards summoning us to the recruiting station. We knew that the Russians gave no training to recruits like us, but just threw us onto the front lines. If we were very lucky we'd come back missing a few limbs. I wanted no part of it. But Jozek wanted to serve. Absolutely. This was his last chance to fight back against the Nazis and he would take it.

My parents, our friends at the Brandwein house, and I all tried to talk sense into him: The war was coming to an end. Why risk everything now? But Jozek wouldn't budge. He was going to battle and that was that. It never really made sense to me. I would come to understand that my brother's decision was driven mainly by heartbreak. He was still in love with Jozia . . . but interfaith marriage was a rare, difficult thing. It could never work. They both knew it. The situation was intolerable to Jozek, especially after having suffered so much loss and deprivation.

I followed him down to the recruiting station and watched through a window as they cut his hair. I took a big chance by sneaking inside to make one final appeal. Maybe I could change his mind and we could both get the hell out of there for good.

Not a chance. He was determined to join the Soviet Army.

I left there in a despondent state, my mind reeling. Jozek would surely be killed on the Russian front. How would my parents ever get over it? What would become of us? And what could I do about any of this? Nothing. Nothing.

I got a job as a procurement agent for the Russian government, acting as a middleman between suppliers and government agencies, brokering deals for the sale and purchase of food and other goods — everything from live cattle to paper notebooks. I also managed to do a little black market business on the side, like everyone else, so I could have a few extra bucks in my pocket. After being in the job for a while, I was able to get my father certified to buy and slaughter live cattle, and deliver the meat to the army or to government warehouses. Of course he did a little side business too — the black market was as much a part of the Communist economy as any other sector.

We carried on day-to-day, waiting for the war to end — we knew it could come at any moment — and praying for Jozek's safe return. After a few weeks, we got a letter from him saying that he'd been wounded. We heard nothing more for a week or so after that, and went wild with anxiety. Finally, a messenger appeared at the Brandweins' front door and gave us the news that Jozek had been shipped to an army hospital in Lvov. My mother and I raced down to see him. When we walked into his room, he was lying covered up to the chest in a blanket. He smiled wanly. Without saying a word, he pulled back his blanket to reveal a grisly war injury: he had lost his leg from the knee down.

Jozek was not able to talk about the accident for many months, but this is the story that eventually emerged:

He had been shipped to the front lines on his first day of service, assigned to a special unit responsible for installing land mines for the Russians and detecting and disarming German mines. They worked with mine-sniffing dogs, but hideous accidents abounded. One day, as Jozek and a few other men were installing mines near a forest south of Krakow — he didn't know where exactly, somewhere in Polish territory — a young man ran across enemy lines and begged for help, miraculously sidestepping freshly laid mines. He was instantly assumed to be a spy, but swore frantically that he was Jewish and knew of many other Jews hiding in the forest who needed to be rescued. Jozek tested him by speaking Yiddish, and when the soldier replied in kind, it was decided that he was telling the truth.

Many areas around the forest were minefields — Jozek knew it well, he had helped lay them — so Jews in hiding would almost surely get blown up on their way out. Jozek and his unit decided to find and rescue the poor souls, and transport them to safety. They carried the terrified civilians one by one across deadly minefields that they themselves had installed. One of the people Jozek carried out of the forest this way was a skinny young lady with fine blond hair. He had gotten her nearly all the way across the danger zone when his foot slipped and — boom! A mine exploded. He managed to toss the girl to safety but didn't remember much after that.

My mother and I wept at the sight of Jozek's disfigurement . . . but also knew how much worse it could be. He'd fought and survived. He was alive. That's what mattered. Now our real lives could begin.

I was in imminent danger of being drafted next, so I decided to migrate to western Poland immediately, with the family to join me soon after. I ran downtown, registered as a Polish citizen, got the proper documents, and in a matter of hours was on my way to Krakow.

The city proved lucky from the start. I arrived on a sunny day in the spring of 1945, and right away bumped into Morris Baum, a good friend of mine from the Brandwein house. He invited me to move into an empty room in the house he was renting. I had a couple of five-ruble gold pieces, which I exchanged for Polish zlotys. The money wouldn't last long.

Everything, especially food, was wildly expensive. I needed an income. As if on cue, I ran into a pair of Russian officers who had just driven down from Germany in a Studebaker truck filled with treifers — odd-lot goods, mostly clothes, shoes, lamps, and household items — that they were looking to sell.

I bought the whole lot with my remaining gold ruble (plus some vodka), and gathered a few local people to sell it off in area markets. The entire truckload sold out in a single day. I was in business.

I bought other truckloads of stuff to sell. Two friends joined me as partners, and soon we were running a profitable operation, sometimes trading in finer fare like jewelry, crystal, and fur. Buyers paid us in Polish zlotys, which we exchanged on the black market for American dollars, thereby adding an extra margin to the profits. In a matter of weeks I was able to move out of Morris's house and get my own apartment in the middle of town, at 23 Swietego Marka, right by the main theater.

When my family joined me in Krakow about six months later, they were amazed at my success. What a joy it was to be able to greet them this way! They moved in with me, and soon my mother was filling the apartment with gorgeous aromas from the kitchen.

I had stopped believing that I would ever experience such simple comforts again, and their sudden re-emergence in my life was disorienting and profoundly moving.

The treifers business fizzled out just as quickly as it had flared up. We searched around for a new, more stable source of money. Jozek, having adjusted remarkably well to the loss of his leg, wore his Russian army uniform everywhere he went — wounded veterans of the Red Army were treated well and generously by all — and soon struck up a friendship with a Russian major. He came home one day with great news: the major had secured for him certain documents that would allow Jozek to travel back and forth over the Hungarian border.

This meant that he could truck in merchandise from Budapest, mostly cigarettes and grapes, both in high demand at the time, and sell it locally at a nice profit. This was totally illegal, of course, but the black market was the only place you could make any real money.

(It was not the first time that Jozek's military uniform had come to the rescue. Months earlier, after I had moved to Krakow but while my family was still living in Lvov, Kazik, the good-hearted young man who, with his lovely girlfriend, had happened upon Jozek and me in the cemetery and stocked us up with much-needed supplies, was arrested by the Russian military police on suspicion that he belonged to a Polish underground resistance group . . . which was probably true. The Russian authorities were about to ship him off to Siberia when Jozek, donned in full military regalia, marched into the security offices where Kazik was being held and told the authorities that the young man had helped save his and his family's lives. The Russians released their prisoner at once — they would not turn a deaf ear to a "war invalid.")

Our new venture was an instant success. There was a bubble in the market for grapes at that time, and at one point Jozek paid two hundred American dollars for three Studebaker truckfuls which we resold to Krakow markets for over six thousand bucks! This was not the norm and the grape market soon collapsed, but overall business remained brisk and steady.

Cigarettes were our staple item, boxes and boxes of cigarettes, the demand for which seemed bottomless. Everybody smoked. Simply everybody. No matter how many cigarettes we smuggled in from Budapest, we'd sell out in no time.

We imposed a limit of a box or two per person, but still couldn't keep pace with demand. Our apartment was constantly jammed with people eager to buy the product in bulk and resell it to local shops at a nice profit. Customers would order and pay at the apartment — my mother handled the money — and the product would be delivered to them later, discreetly, by truck. We worked with a guy who operated a few trucks for black market purposes like this.

He outsmarted the cops by keeping the trucks constantly on the move, never parking them in the same place twice . . . and equipping each truck with several tarps of different colors. If a driver suspected that a cop had spotted him, he'd pull his truck into a secluded area, switch out the tarp, and return to business. The whole operation was quite bold. In that time and place, what else could it be?

One Sunday afternoon, I was strolling down the street in the middle of town with two girls I'd known for a while — a new normal seemed to be establishing itself in our lives — when I spied a young girl walking in the opposite direction, loaded down with heavy suitcases. As we got closer, I recognized her.

Dora Schrank!

She'd missed her scheduled transport to Palestine and the next one would not leave for several weeks or more. She had just arrived in Krakow — had literally just gotten off a train — and was on her way to a Jewish organization to seek help.

What were the chances that I would run into her at just this moment? It was astonishing. I grabbed her bags and led her home to our apartment. My mother was overjoyed at the sight of her and insisted that Dora move in. We were already five people sharing a one-bedroom flat — a cousin of my father's had recently resurfaced — so what was one more? We made an extra bed, laid another plate at the dinner table, and Dora became part of the family. She was around fifteen years old at that time, and I was just about twenty. It would be a while yet before I allowed myself to notice what a fine and beautiful young woman she was becoming. I can't pinpoint the moment we fell in love. All I know is that it happened eventually ... and when it did, it felt like the most natural thing in the world.

Our apartment became a hub of news, information, and stories of survival.

"We have company," my mother announced one day, in typical fashion, as I crossed the threshold. A young lady sat perched on the couch, smiling, with a young man at her side.

"Recognize her?" asked my mother. I didn't.

"You really don't remember me?" asked the woman.

At the sound of her voice I almost fainted. Of course I knew this woman. It was Anna Mantel, our old friend and neighbor. Her brother Aron and I had been good buddies, active together in school and sports. The SS had killed their father, a quiet, devoutly religious man with a long traditional beard, in the most brutal way. He was a glazier by trade and was repairing some windows on a private house when a truck carrying Jews to the Piaski passed by. One of the prisoners tried to escape by jumping off the truck, and was immediately shot dead. Mr. Mantel was ordered under threat of death to drag the body back to the truck. He did so, and then the SS beat him nearly to death and tossed him onto the truck as well.

Anna had survived by posing as a Christian. The young man sitting next to her was her boyfriend, who had only recently learned the truth. Anna's sister Ita had also managed to escape and survive in the same fashion. She'd been married to a doctor for several years now and they had a couple of children. He still had no idea that she was Jewish.

"Right after the war," Anna told us, "I sat my boyfriend down. 'I'm not a Catholic,' I said. 'I'm a Jew. You can go now and look for a real Christian girlfriend.'"

(Anna looked pretty Jewish to me. And her accent was so strong that other Jewish girls used to laugh at her and imitate the sound of it. How was it possible that she had been able to pass?)

"But he didn't care," the lucky girl continued. "He said, 'I love you and I want to be with you for the rest of my life.' Isn't that beautiful? Isn't he handsome?"

The shy fellow blushed and wriggled in his seat. My mother embraced them and insisted they stay for dinner. We passed a pleasant evening together. I never saw Anna or the young man again after that. I often wonder what became of them.

The regular customers of our cigarette business came to love my mother in a special way. She always had time to listen to their tales, always tried to lend a helping hand. A sweet young girl named Rozia Lesser and her mother, Helen, were particular favorites. Sole survivors of their extended family, they'd gotten some help along the way from a man who had since followed them to Krakow and was now after Rozia in the worst way. She wanted nothing to do with him but he kept coming around, stalking the girl and making life miserable.

Rozia's mother showed up at the apartment one morning alone, and sobbed out an ugly story. The stalker had broken into their apartment the night before and beaten Rozia mercilessly. He screamed that she belonged to him since he saved her life, and vowed to beat her like this every day until she agreed to marry him. The mother was in a panic. They had survived the war to endure this hell? My mother urged her to bring Rozia around, and the next day the poor girl showed up at our door. Her face was bruised, cut and covered in bandages, injured so severely that she could barely speak.

I happened to be in the apartment at the time, along with a partner of ours named Motie. When we saw the beating that creep had given her and heard the whole story, Motie and I exchanged a knowing look.

Motie (left) and me in Krakow, 1946. Motie was a Resistance fighter during the War.

We knew what we had to do. I owned a couple of guns, a Russian Vis and a tiny German pistol, and I knew Motie owned one too.

"You have it with you?" I asked.

"Of course," he said. "I don't go anywhere without it."

I asked Rozia if she knew where we could find the stalker.

"By the Sukiennice," she warbled through her bandages, referring to a great plaza marketplace where dollars, gold, jewelry, vodka, and other such commodities were traded.

We asked her to come with us so she could point him out, and the three of us walked down Floriańska Street until we came to the Sukiennice.

We hadn't even circled halfway around the place when she spotted him. Motie and I strode over to the guy, Rozia in the middle. I got very close, pulled out my Vis, and whispered to him in Polish.

"If you ever hit this girl again or do anything to scare or hurt her, if you so much as glance in her direction, I will come back and fill your head and chest with every bullet in this gun."

And I meant it. After all I had seen, what was one more life? I could have wasted him right there and not batted an eye. Motie really wanted to pull the trigger.

"He deserves it," he said. "Look at what he did to her."

The punk was terrified. He stared at us with unblinking eyes, his face white as paper, and vowed to comply. Rozia never saw him again after that.

It was the spring of 1946. I had been living in Krakow for a year. My favorite nightclub was a place called Fenix, on Florianka Street, just a couple of blocks from our apartment, where my friends and I went so often that we had a regular table. (It was over drinks at Fenix, in fact, that Jozek finally told me the story of how he lost his leg.) I asked my parents to join me there one Saturday night to see a live program that I knew they'd enjoy. To my surprise, they said yes.

"Can I bring Rozia?" Mother asked.

"Of course," I replied eagerly. It was a particular pleasure, quite rare, to see my parents relax and enjoy themselves. Jozek had made other plans that night so he couldn't join us. I lined up a date for the evening, met up with a bunch of other friends, and the whole lot of us headed out to the club on foot, as usual. We walked into the place with an easy swagger and took our usual table. The manager sailed over with a tray of drinks. A live band was playing "Bei Mir Bist Du Shein." We were in good spirits.

My father sat at the end of the table. Next to him, my mother and Rozia huddled together and talked into each other's ears the whole night. I offered to take Rozia for a spin on the dance floor a few times, but she would not break away. Eventually, I saw my mother reach into her pocketbook and take out a photograph.

"That's him!" Rozia screamed. "That's the soldier who carried me across the minefield! He's the reason I'm still alive!"

It was Jozek.

In an uncanny twist of fate, Rozia was the young girl he had been carrying when he stepped on that landmine and lost his leg!

Mother and Rozia went practically hysterical. When we told Jozek about it he was skeptical, but then he met Rozia and remembered her immediately. He had branched out into selling other kinds of goods and was not part of our day-to-day cigarette operation, so he'd never seen her before. Now he couldn't get enough of the girl. It was good to see my brother begin to recover from his lingering heartbreak over Jozia. He had been more deeply in love with her than we knew. A

Polish Catholic friend of my mother's, a fine, respectable woman, devoutly religious, confessed that Jozek had come to her in the months before he signed up for the army for advice about converting to Christianity. He wanted to marry Jozia, he explained, and this was the only way. The woman counseled against it.

"You were born Jewish, you should die Jewish," she said. Jozek went back to her several times, but eventually gave up on the idea.

My mother, father and I discussed the story amongst ourselves, but didn't breathe a word of it to Jozek. It was all in the past, water under the bridge. Why re-open the wound — especially now that he was becoming smitten with Rozia? They started going out almost every night, and she was constantly at our house. Pretty soon, it seemed like they were falling in love.

But it was not to be.

On July 4, 1946, less than a year after the war ended, violence erupted at a Jewish community center in Kielce, about a hundred kilometers north of Krakow, and exploded into the street.

A bloodthirsty mob rampaged wildly through town, beating and murdering Jews with abandon. They claimed that Jews had killed a Christian boy and used his blood to make matzo — that ancient vicious trope. Forty or more innocent Jews were slaughtered that day. The world reacted with horror to the Kielce Pogrom, as it would become known, and Polish authorities feigned outrage. But we knew better. Poland was under the Russian hammer and that was that.

It wasn't going to change anytime soon. Our country had become one big cemetery for Jews.

We went to Breslau and filed for permission to resettle in the American zone across the border in

Germany. Within days, our papers were in order and we fled to Munich, along with thousands of other Jews; it was an exodus.

Jozek and Rozia would be reunited years later, in America … but by then they'd be leading very different lives.

Chapter Thirteen

~~~

Munich had taken extensive bombing during the war, so apartments were scarce, as were jobs and food. Thankfully, we had a saved little money . . . and encountered another stroke of luck.

An officer in the City Apartment Control office, a German Jew named Mr. Levi, took a liking to me and went out of his way to help us get an apartment in a fine neighborhood called Ramersdorf — a spacious two-bedroom at Anziger Strasse 12, with a big kitchen and sunny veranda. It was like hitting the lottery. Then this good man, a stranger to whom I shall always be grateful, helped me get a license to open a kosher meat market — a real coup, especially since food was carefully rationed in Germany at that time. I built a shop on Kirchenstrasse and suddenly we were in the meat business again, my parents, Jozek, and I.

Meat had been my father's trade all his life, as it had his father's before him, and his before that. And it would become mine. But the truth is I never liked it. The blood and gore always disturbed me. Now, after all the savagery I'd witnessed, I was barely able to stomach the sights and smells — dead cows and calves split wide open, hanging upside down with their insides ripped out, their flesh being carved away from the bone. I had always found this revolting, but it was worse now. Even as a child, my father's butcher shop was a place I tried to avoid. I passed it on my way home from school and my mother often complained that I never stepped inside.

"How can you walk by like that and not come in and say hello?"

I never told her the real reason.

The slaughterhouse, which my father took me to a couple of times when I was very young, was for me the stuff of nightmares. I could sense fear and terror in the eyes and bodies of all those innocent creatures lined up for the kill, hear anguish in their cries, practically understand their pleas.

"Help me! Save me! Don't kill my babies!"

And I hated the ritual slaughter of chickens in the backyard of our synagogue. Women carried birds back there to be killed in proper kosher fashion by the szlachta, overseen by our rabbi. The wriggling, squawking creatures, the szlachta's knife at their throats, the cutting, the blood . . . I wanted no part of it.

But meat was our livelihood. And we were lucky to have one. You learn to suck it up. There is no choice. I donned my bloody apron and set to work, deeply grateful to kind Mr. Levi for giving us this fresh start.

Dora had moved with us to Munich, of course, but she and I weren't romantically involved. I was attracted to her, yes, but the age difference and the fact that we were living together as siblings made things complicated. It was best to go slowly.

We made a good living with the butcher shop, and before long my father was able to buy a used Škoda and even hire a driver, a German man named Franz. I bought a couple of cars of my own — a pair of used Opel 2-litres in dark blue, one a convertible. Only one of the cars was registered, so I slapped the single license plate onto whichever car I was driving. I learned the subtle tricks of dealing with ration cards and all the other bureaucracy, and figured out how to wrangle an import license so I could start shipping in live cattle to slaughter, and sell the meat to hospitals, schools, and other large institutions.

Always in the front of our minds were Staszek, Kasia, and their family. We owed them everything, everything. It was our top priority to stay in regular contact with them and send money every month, but both proved challenging. There were no direct phone lines or other open communications between West Germany and Russian-occupied eastern Poland, and cross-border postal services were unreliable at best.

We discovered there existed an underground network of couriers, mostly Jews from western Poland who had been in concentration camps until they were liberated by American forces. They'd spent time living in the American zone and felt quite at home among the Yankees. Many of them spoke fluent English. This was all quite exotic to us — we had never even met an American — but a lot of these folks seemed good and honest, so we decided to take a chance.

We wrote newsy letters to the Niedziolkas, stuffed the envelopes with cash, put them into the pipeline . . . and hoped for the best.

We sent American dollars — they were in high demand, very valuable on the black market. Just a single American dollar could buy a nice load of food and other supplies, and we sent fifty or a hundred at once, substantial sums of money in those years.

We'd often receive confirmation that our packages had arrived safely. But many times we had no idea. In the end, we discovered that nearly every penny we ever sent the Niedziolkas had reached its destination.

Life in Munich proceeded at a busy clip, with

the butcher shop running at high gear and a social life beginning to form for Jozek and me. Strange how quickly present tense reality can eclipse even the freshest horror. I was surprised by how little I found myself reflecting on everything we'd just endured. It was never really far beneath the surface, but I didn't dwell on it. I had just turned twenty-one and made a bunch of new friends, mostly other Jewish boys around my age. We went out together on weekends in a big group to frolic in Munich's nightlife scene — hot spots seemed to pop up out of nowhere all the time.

As I was sipping a drink in a nightclub one Saturday night, I forget the name of the place, just watching people spin around the dance floor, I spotted a familiar face across the room: Abe Baum, a young guy I knew from the Brandwein house. What a treat to see him. I had often wondered where my friends from those days ended up. We made our way toward each other across the crowded joint, shouted eager greetings over the noise, and made a date to get together for dinner.

A few nights later, Abe, Jozek, and I caught up on everything over a big meal at a local restaurant — the hideous past, yes, but mostly the present. Abe told us that he and many of our friends and acquaintances from the Jewish House were now living in a Displaced Persons (DP) camp in Kassel, Germany. They were well cared for, he said, and free from harm.

"Oh, and I met someone who says he knows you and your family," Abe burbled cheerfully. "Told me to say hello. A guy named Buc Scherzer. Remember him?"

Buc Scherzer.

Time stopped. I asked Abe to describe him.

"Chubby guy, blonde hair, reddish face. Real

happy-go-lucky type." Jozek and I looked at each other. A tense silence gripped the table.

"What's going on?" Abe asked nervously. "Did I do something wrong here?"

"He was a spy!" I blurted out, then lowered my voice and told Abe the story:

Buc was from Lvov, and though Jozek and I had known him only in passing and hadn't seen him in several years, we heard from reliable sources that he had worked as a secret agent for the Gestapo during the war, exposing Jews posing as Christians, and came to be considered a highly valuable asset by the Nazis. There was a special place in hell for execrable traitors like Buc Scherzer, who sold their souls to the devil for a song and willingly sentenced their own friends and neighbors, their own people, to torture and death.

Abe was badly shaken up. He left Munich after a few days but said he planned to return before long. Jozek and I spoke to an old friend of ours from Lvov, Lonek Kaczenos, one of a small handful of survivors from our former lives — and we all agreed that the traitor must not continue to live. Lonek announced that he would perform the execution himself. I think he wanted to spare Jozek and me the act of spilling another man's blood, but I think also he wanted the chance to kill a Nazi spy.

"Where do I find him?" he demanded, his eyes growing feral.

I urged him to do nothing on his own. We would do it together or not at all. He fought me hard on this but finally relented. We agreed that we'd confront Buc as a group. I had left my two guns in Poland and tried to get my hands on another. Lonek wouldn't hear of it. He had a gun. He'd pull the trigger. On that point he would not budge.

A few weeks passed before Abe came back to Munich. We didn't tell him what we were planning, but urged him to bring Buc next time he visited.

"Tell him we want to see him so we can clear the air. It's probably all just a big misunderstanding. If he comes here we can get it straightened out."

A few days later, Abe was back . . . with Buc Scherzer in tow.

"He's right down there," he told us, "sitting in that café on the corner."

My palms went clammy. I summoned Jozek and Lonek, and the three of us walked down the block in edgy silence.

There was the café, steps away, red awning, big plate glass window. The rat was on the other side of that glass.

Our plan was to chat with him a while, lure him out to an isolated spot, and do the deed. We walked through the front door of the place with thrashing hearts. The blood ran cold in my veins. Buc was sitting alone at a table with his back to us. I called out his name. He turned to face me. And I almost fainted.

Wrong guy! This was a different Buc Scherzer!

This Buc was one of Jozek's fellow drivers at the Janowska camp. He lived in the stables with all the other kutchers, and was cheerful and generous whenever I snuck in to visit, always passing me little gifts and treats, trying to buck up my spirit.

We never knew his last name, though he knew ours because my parents ran the kitchen. By some bizarre coincidence, he bore a striking physical resemblance to his traitorous namesake. It was a simple case of mistaken identity.

"Ludwig! Jozek!" Buc cried, and jumped to his feet to give us a hug. We lurched toward him, laughing and maybe crying a little too. Lonek looked on in utter confusion.We passed a wonderful day together, laughing and reminiscing over drinks and sandwiches, grateful to our bones that we had not let Lonek go out alone to kill this innocent man, a fellow survivor.

A chance to seek legitimate justice arrived soon after.

The German government announced that it had arrested several SS men and was looking for Jewish survivors of Nazi concentration camps in and around Lvov to serve as witnesses. I registered as a survivor of the Janowska camp and received a card to appear at court to testify against a murderer in uniform named Melhor.

Melhor. I remembered him well. Still do. I remember every name and face. You never forget these people.

I took the stand and bore witness against Melhor, cataloguing his crimes and calling out other torturers and mass murderers — especially the Commandants of Janowska, Wilhaus and Gebauer, who, like so many others, had managed to escape.

And I spoke up for the SS man Caulke, who was so kind and gentle, an angel of mercy who helped us in countless ways. Some hapless souls ended up in SS not really knowing what they were getting into, and once there quickly devolved into monsters. Not Caulke. He retained his essential goodness and humanity, and did his best to help the prisoners in his charge do the same.

"If you ever find him," I urged, "thank him for us. And reward him."

I walked home that day with my face to the sun, a breeze at my back.

My family and I remained in Munich for a few years more, planning all the while to emigrate to the U.S.A. We would not be able to make the voyage as a family — visas were issued in a seemingly random order, and you had to move quickly once called. Only husbands and wives were guaranteed passage together.

My parents were summoned in the spring of 1949, and their passage arranged. Jozek and I waved goodbye to them from the dock with joy and grief mingling in our hearts — being separated like this was still terrifying, no matter how good the reason.

My visa was issued a few weeks later. On a cloudy morning in the middle of May, I set sail aboard the General Stuart, a small but nicely appointed Army boat filled with survivors, mostly Jews but also some Gentiles. It was an extremely rough passage. There were times the little vessel felt like a mere toy upon the raging sea. Up and down it crashed for days at a stretch, sometimes smashing so deep into the surf that I didn't think it would come back up again. But on May 30, 1949 — Decoration Day, as it turns out — I arrived safely on American shores.

I remember people weeping as we sailed into New York Harbor, others praying or making the sign of the cross. I just stared in slack-jawed awe at the Manhattan skyline as it swelled and expanded in my field of vision until it seemed to engulf me completely.

My parents greeted me joyfully at the dock, bundled me into a waiting car, and drove me out to Borough Park, Brooklyn where they were living with my father's brother and his wife, who'd moved to

America in 1921.

Dora was next to arrive. Her ship would come in at Boston Harbor, so my cousin Nat Kalt, his wife Fay, and I drove up there to fetch her.

Nat and Fay. How warmly they embraced us, how beautifully they treated us, with such kindness and generosity, during our earliest days in America! (Nat's sister and her husband, Violet and Clarence Gudinsky, were equally good to us.)

The relief and gladness I felt upon laying eyes on Dora again was bone-deep. We were in love by then. It had happened sometime during our years in Munich; it's hard to say exactly when. Hadn't we always been in love? Hadn't I loved her like this since the day we sat in her empty house and shared the hope that her father might miraculously return? And yet I don't think I grasped the full depth of my feeling for this beautiful young woman, my soul mate, until our reunion on American shores.

It was in the New World that our love fully bloomed.

Dora and I were married on August 7, 1949 in a small but tender ceremony. We moved into a rented apartment near my aunt and uncle's house — Borough Park was filling up fast with other Polish and Russian Jews in those days. On June 15th of the following year, Dora gave birth to our first son, Nat, named for his maternal grandfather. Our second son, Michael, was born in 1954 . . . and soon we were just another hard-working immigrant family, part of the great melting pot.

Dora and me with our sons Nat (foreground)
and Michael, around 1957

The Trial, Part 2: Eye to Eye

~~~

As I turned away from the model of the Janowska Camp and Dora and I began to leave the courtroom, our interpreters — an earnest woman in her twenties and a quiet man around my age — asked if they could join us for lunch. Both were pleasant and respectful, and I was fluent enough in German to know that they had translated my testimony faithfully. Dora and I readily agreed, and the four of us went to a nearby coffee shop.

Over sandwiches and coffee, the young woman asked a lot of questions and seemed eager to extract as much detail as possible, especially about Gebauer's crimes. I could see that many of our answers pained her deeply. She hardly touched her food. Why was she pushing so hard? What was she after? The whole thing started to feel oppressive.

"I have a question for you," I said at last, almost just to change the subject, "if you don't mind."

"Please, please," she said.

"What should the world make of you Germans? How can the world ever trust you again? Hundreds of thousands of people had to cooperate in order for so many millions to be murdered. What kind of people did that? How can history forgive them?"

She nodded gravely, didn't answer right away.

"I don't know. But it's what Germans are discussing at the dinner table every night. Many in the younger generation reject their parents' excuses. It's tearing families apart."

The male interpreter regarded his female colleague thoughtfully but said nothing. We sat quietly for a moment. There was so much to say and no way to say it. Best to let silence fill the breach. We paid the bill and headed back to the courtroom.

Gebauer never took the stand and his attorneys mounted practically no defense at all. They seemed almost to be arguing for the prosecution.

We carried on with various legal formalities — I signed a number of documents and answered a few more questions — and then new evidence was introduced, some damning documents from Janowska bearing Gebauer's signature. A great fuss was made. The papers were a smoking gun.

When it was all over, a young man stopped Dora and me on our way out of the courtroom. He was about twenty, exceedingly courteous and well dressed. I assumed he was one of the many college students who had attended the trial.

Then he identified himself: Fritz Gebauer's son.

He ignored me completely, addressed Dora directly. He asked if she were a survivor, and, if so, why she hadn't taken the stand, almost challenging her on this point.

"Did my father really do all the things everyone testified about? How is it possible? I don't know him to be that kind of a man at all."

He gazed at Dora with a beseeching look, desperate to hear . . . what? That it was all a lie? I was tempted to jump in and answer first but didn't know where to begin. Dora just regarded him for a moment and then responded simply, with something much better than anything I could have offered.

"Do you think all these people would travel from all over the world, leave their families and children and businesses behind, to accuse an innocent man? Why would they do that? Go to Lvov if you still doubt it. Speak to the people there. They remember your father. They know what he and Wilhaus did."

The young man's face appeared to crack. He looked sick. He seemed to want to say something more, but then waved his hand and stumbled away.

I felt for him. He was blameless. He imagined his father to be an upstanding citizen, a solid family man. Maybe Fritz had coached his son's soccer team or volunteered at church. Maybe he had taught the boy to ride a bike or tie a tie. The young man's world was collapsing around him.

I considered calling him back. But what would I say? He was intelligent, educated, and knew well the recent history of his country. Had he never had a clue that his father was a notorious Nazi criminal? Had he never questioned his father about the war years? Had he believed every lie he must have been told?

The mind is capable of great trickery, so I'm willing to imagine that the young man simply blinded himself to the signs that must have been everywhere in an unconscious effort to avoid the agony of facing the truth. It doesn't change the fact that he was innocent.

And yet this young man's veins flowed with the blood of a Nazi murderer. I felt no desire to speak gently to that blood or warm it in the hold of my hand. I wanted only for this young man to walk away changed, forever, by the truth.

Fritz Gebauer left the courthouse that day the same way he'd arrived: In a sports car, unshackled and at ease. He was ultimately found guilty on all counts and, in 1971, sentenced to life in prison. His lawyers filed an appeal to overturn the conviction, which was rejected by the German Supreme Court on July 24, 1972.

Gebauer died in 1979, eight years after being convicted, and during that time not a day went by that I didn't draw satisfaction from knowing that I had helped bare his filthy truth to the world.

The passage of time has done little to shed light or understanding on the likes of Fritz Gebauer or the Nazi phenomenon in general.

It remains inexplicable to me, and stands alone in human history.

Genocide exists in every era and in many places around the world — as Jews we should scream from the nearest mountaintop wherever and whenever we see it — but the particulars of Nazism put it a class unto itself: the invention and use of sophisticated machinery and technology in the service of mass murder; the near total manipulation and control of the masses; the public spectacle and drama, the majesty and glory of state in which Nazism draped itself; its ability to awaken in hundreds of thousands of average citizens a primitive bloodlust fueled by bottomless rage and marked by an eager willingness to surrender their souls to something that can rightly be called the Devil.

It seems to me that you have to reach into ancient history to find anything of its ilk — the Roman Coliseum, perhaps, the Spanish Inquisition, the Crusades. There, too, you had epically well-produced spectacle in the service of the most brutal human acts imaginable, and a corrupted populace yearning to eat it up.

If a memoir like this has any value at all, and I pray it does, it is in part to awaken and re-awaken the reader to the depths of evil to which human beings are capable of sinking . . . and to inspire and renew the eternal drive to defeat it.

Epilogue

~~~

People often ask what I think made it possible for my family and I to survive. I'm never sure how to answer. Hope played a part, certainly — without hope, why strive and struggle? And luck, lots of luck. Common sense didn't hurt. Nor did youth. Jozek and I shared a proud, defiant spirit. We were rebels at heart, and that gave us a certain advantage. So many people in the Ghetto and later, in the camp, clung to the belief that they would survive if only they cooperated and kept their noses clean, their profiles low. Jozek and I knew in our youthful kishkes that this was not the way to go, knew that we had to be wily and proactive, knew that complacency was death. Plus we were too proud to bow to those Nazi perverts.

More than anything, though, our survival was possible because the winds of fortune blew into our path so many good people who were willing to risk their lives to save ours. If there is a G-d, surely He led us to the Niedziolka family.

Our clans remain closely bound to this day. For seventy years and more I have devoted myself to helping and supporting the Niedziolkas, their children, grandchildren, and great grandchildren in every way possible. Dora and I were heartbroken when Staszek died of cancer in the spring of 1960. Later that same year, Vladek, the third oldest Niedziolka child, fell deathly ill. We had no intention of losing him, too. The doctors in Poland knew of only one drug that might help, available only in America. The medication proved elusive, its procurement complicated, but I hunted it down, drove out to Kennedy Airport, and personally put it on a plane bound for Poland.

Vladek responded well to the treatment and soon recovered. I would have done nearly anything to help save his life; that I was able to do so makes me proud and grateful beyond words.

Dora and I hosted many members of the Niedziolka clan for months at a time over the years . . . but the most meaningful visit of all came in 1963, when Kasia traveled to America for the first and only time in her life to attend the Bar Mitzvah of our oldest son, Nat.

We did not want to celebrate this solemn rite of passage without her. There was some trouble with her visa arrangements, so we appealed to a local congressman for help. He contacted the Consul in Warsaw, and soon Kasia was on her way.

The five Niedziolka siblings at home in Poland during the mid-1980s.
From left to right: Romek, Broner, Zosia, Vladek and Jozia

There she stood at the candle-lighting ceremony to give her blessing to the Bar Mitzvah boy . . . who would never have been born had not this woman saved his father's life, not once but over and over again. The room went silent as she lit the candle. A photographer captured the iconic moment. That single image says more than all the words I could possibly conjure to describe it.

Dora and I celebrated our fiftieth wedding anniversary on August 7, 1999 with a big party at the

Kasia lighting the 13th candle at Nat's Bar Mitzvah

National in Brighton Beach. All our friends and family were there . . . including Vladek and Hanka Niedziolka. The local press reported on the event as a human-interest story, which in turn got picked up by a few national news outlets. Our fifteen minutes of fame, I guess. (The story would surface in the news again a few years later, in 2002, when the Israeli government hosted a great ceremony in Poland to honor the Niedziolka family and other righteous Gentiles.)

The anniversary party was a bittersweet affair.

Dora had been sick for several years by then, frail and full of pain, her condition worsening every week. Nothing seemed to help. In 2004, she suffered a debilitating stroke from which she never fully recovered. She died four years later, on March 7, 2008.

My wife and I were friends above all. It had always been that way. Friends. Cut from the same piece of cloth. We saw things the same way, believed in the same things, shared the same lives. We belonged together, completed each other. Lou and Dora. Dora and Lou. A single entity. She's been dead for seven years at the time of this writing, and yet I talk to her every day.

Dora and me on our 50th wedding anniversary

Dora never wanted to discuss the past. Whenever I tried to engage her in direct conversation about it, she'd change the subject. For years, I'd been able to talk about the Holocaust only with other survivors, never at home. But on a visit to the Holocaust Memorial Museum in Washington, D.C. in the early 1990s, Dora began to open up for the first time, whispering memories into my ear as we moved past artifacts and exhibits as if viewing life on another planet. Later, as we sat in the museum café, I asked what had taken her so long. She told me that soon after we arrived in America, she became friendly with an American-born Jewish woman who advised her never to talk about the Holocaust.

Dora and one of the children she looked after at the yeast factory, 1944

"It's too disturbing," the woman told her. "We don't want to hear about it." Dora took those words to heart . . . and remained silent for decades.

"I wanted to have friends," she said.

It's our turn to fade into history, we who lived the stories I've remembered here. My father died of cancer in 1965. My mother died twenty years later. Jozek passed away in 1996. Staszko and Kasia are long gone. Henek, Falik, Michael, and the others, so many, are all deceased. But from these pages and for all time our voices cry out:

Remember! Remember!

 HONOR ROLL

Seventeen righteous Gentiles who risked everything to save my life and the lives of my parents, brother, and others:

Misko Niedziolka, that most gentle soul, who secured a safe hiding place for my family on his brother's farm and stayed close to us throughout the War years and beyond.

Grzesko, the Ukrainian policemen, a friend of my father's — I never knew his last name — who disguised my parents as Ukrainian peasants and safely guided them out of the closed Ghetto and beyond city limits on foot.

Staszko Czudowski, who smuggled letters to and from my parents and kept us closely apprised of their safety and whereabouts while Jozek and I were still imprisoned at Janowska Concentration Camp.

The young Polish Catholic driver who helped my brother, Henek, and me escape Janowska. His name is lost to history, I'm sorry to say, but without his help our survival would not have been possible.

Staszek (Staszko) and Katarzyna (Kasia) Niedziolka, who hid us in the attic of their humble barn and, later, in an underground bunker on their property, and whose efforts on our behalf were tireless, fearless, and utterly lifesaving. Never have I known more loyal friends and protectors, or nobler spirits.

The six Niedziolka children (in age order): Kazik, Józka, Vladek, Broner, Zosia, and Romek, who embraced us as family, were so tender and sweet to us throughout our time in hiding . . . and who guarded well the secret of our presence despite their youth and inexperience.

Babcia Niedziolka, Staszko's mother, who from the first night Jozek, Henek, and I escaped from Janowska and huddled in a dark room of her house, showered us with motherly love and devotion despite the fact that we were total strangers — a truly remarkable woman whose capacity to love and nurture was seemingly limitless.

Stasia, Kasia's niece, a luminous soul who seemed to light up the pitch black bunker whenever she came to see us, always bearing gifts and kind words, stirring joy and hope in our hearts despite the unrelenting bleakness of our existence.

Michael, indomitable Michael, who leapt at every task like a hungry lion, mastered whatever he set his hand to, always thought several steps ahead. His ingenuity and industriousness were critical to our survival; his easy smile and open heart, a salve for our souls.

Zosia and Dziunka Polakowa, who guarded our secret fiercely, and did everything in their power to bring comfort, peace — and even a little fun! — into our lives throughout our time in hiding.

Bless them.

Bless them all.

COURT TRANSCRIPT

What follows is a translation from German to English of the official transcript of my testimony at the criminal trial of Fritz Gebauer in Saarbrücken, Germany on December 7, 1970. The transcript has been buried in archival storage for decades, and appears here for the first time in print.

The format of this document has been reproduced in these pages exactly as it appears in the original, with the sole addition of parentheses and line spaces to separate stenographic notations from actual testimony. A few minor liberties have been taken with grammar and usage for the sake of readability.

The reader will note that the name Charatan is misspelled in the transcript as Sharatan.

There are several other errors as well, mostly minor, all of which are corrected and discussed in the Comments and Corrections section immediately following the transcript.

Witness Sharatan was called and was heard with the aid of an interpreter. He states as follows:

3. Witness:

a) Personal data:

S h a r a t a n Ludwig, born on 08.25.1925 in Lemberg, butcher by trade, residing in Brooklyn/ USA, is neither related to the defendant nor related by marriage.

b) Relating to the matter:

In the summer of 1942 I was arrested in the ghetto and brought to the central work camp (ZAL). I cannot tell you today for how long I was held and worked there until I was transferred to the Deutsche Ausrüstungswerke (DAW). I do recall that I spent about half a year in the DAW and late in the summer of 1943, I was able to escape. I had worked earlier for the Schwarz Company while living in the ghetto as a mechanic and doing ironing, before the Schwarz company was acquired by DAW and they had me do the same at DAW.

I remember exactly the day when the night shift at the Schwarz Company was brought to the work camp and was killed. It was March 30, 1943. My sister was one of the people who worked at Schwarz and had to do the night shift on this day. I recognized my sister's clothes later at the place where the clothes were collected. I was told that Gebauer and Willhaus were responsible for the shootings... [UNINTELLIGIBLE END OF SENTENCE.]

I got to know him when I was working in the DAW. I worked in the ironing barracks, which had two floors. On one floor was the ironing room and on the other floor other items were manufactured.

(A model was erected in the court room, and like all other parties to the action, the witness pointed out the entrance to the work camp, the office of Achser, the entrance to DAW, the administration building of the work camp and the barracks in which the witness had worked.)

During my work period in DAW, I have witnessed the following:

On a very cold day at New Year 1942/1943, Gebauer arranged for a barrel to be filled with water. Inmates had to get undressed and had to immerse themselves into the barrel of water. I remember that one inmate had tried to hold his head above the water. Gebauer ordered that they had to immerse themselves fully into the water, including their heads. They did as they were ordered. These inmates died later due to pneumonia. I have seen this with my own eyes. On another occasion, Gebauer caught one guy smoking a cigarette, which was not permitted. This was most likely at the end of 1942. I was near the ironing room, but standing outside. The distance to them was about three times the length of this courtroom.

(The witness points to both ends of the courtroom. The courtroom is approx. 30 meters long.)

Gebauer kicked the inmate and he fell to the ground. He stepped on his throat until he was dead.

Ludwig Charatan

In 1943 and I am certain, because I fled soon after in the summer of that year, I witnessed another case in which Gebauer killed an inmate. This inmate had to dig sand with a shovel; however, Gebauer did not like his efforts. He showed the inmate how much sand had to go on the shovel. This incident happened across the street from my workshop, because a foundation for a new workshop was under construction. As to the question how Gebauer was killing the inmates, I have to answer the following: he always used the same method of murdering: Gebauer would hit the inmates over the head and step on their throats. One Saturday, we were mustered and the SS men Gebauer, Malchior, Müller and Röhrig were present. Prior to that, we received the order that all inmates with children must bring them along to the mustering ground.

All children were loaded on a so-called wooden carriage and driven to Piaski. That is my assumption, and I have never seen the children again.

Now, I am presented with my testimony made before the Consulate General of the Federal Republic of Germany in New York on 03.04.1963. It states that when a woman tried to prevent her child from being taken, she was also selected.

I confirm that this is true and I still have memory of that.

(For purpose of caveat, the sworn statement of the witness, which he stated before the Central Committee of Liberated Jews in Munich on 01.30.1948 is read aloud.)

The witness declares:

I can recall this statement, which was recorded at that time and it is true.

Witness declares further:

I recall another incident in the DAW, when Gebauer had killed an inmate.

Gebauer hired a woman to work in the department, in which the clothes of killed Jews were

collected. The woman had to get
fully naked while searching for
valuable things hidden in the
clothes. She had to get undressed
so that she would not be able
to hide any jewelry in her work
clothes. However, she must
have done so. She had hidden a
valuable thing in her hair and
Gebauer was notified about that.
There was a rumor going around in
the DAW. Gebauer ordered gallows
to be built, and when they were
erected we were mustered by
Gebauer.

Before the woman was hanged on
the gallows, Gebauer kicked her
and he strangled her.

In this connection, I recall the
question of the chairman whether
I had witnessed an execution in
the DAW. I remember this and
witnessed this myself, since I
was mustered at the time.

The witness was sworn in. He took
an oath wearing a hat.

b. u. v.

The hearing is interrupted and

will be continued on
December 10, 1970. at 9.00am

Signature   Signature

Remarks: The minutes of this
meeting were made on 12.07.70.

Comments and Corrections to the Transcript

My testimony was given in English, with a Polish accent, to a German-speaking court; it was simultaneously translated into German by court interpreters and recorded, probably by hand, by a court stenographer. Now, forty-four years later, it has been translated back into English. This circuitous linguistic route — together with the German custom of taking "minutes" during a trial, as opposed to making a word-for-word stenographic record — is likely the reason that a few words might sound out of character.

The use of the words "muster," "mustered," and "mustering," for example, are clearly substitutes for whatever words I actually used to describe the relevant events. I might have said something like, "They called us all into the yard and made us line up in military formation," correctly identified by the court stenographer as having been "mustered," and recorded as such in the transcript.

Also, on the fifth page of the transcript, the following phrase appears (underlined words are underlined in the original):

"Now, I <u>am presented</u> with my testimony made before the Consulate General of the Republic of Germany in New York on 01.01.1963."

This statement should probably have been written in the second person, as in: "Now, the witness <u>is presented</u> with his testimony made before the Consulate General of the Republic of Germany in New York on 01.01.1963."

There are three other errors, more substantive, that I hasten to correct.

The first sentence of my recorded testimony reads as follows:

"In the summer of 1942 I was arrested in the ghetto and brought to the central work camp (ZAL). I cannot tell you today for how long I was held and worked there until I was transferred to the Deutsche Ausrüstungswerke (DAW).

I was never arrested and brought to the ZAL. The work camp known as the Jüdisches Zwangsarbeitslager, or ZAL, was located in the Rzeszow ghetto, a good distance away from Lvov. The most likely explanation for this error is that the detail accidentally migrated into my testimony from that of another survivor's; indeed, the testimony of a man named Rosen appears in the court transcript immediately before my own, with no clear separation between our sections other than a single line break.

The transcript appears to confuse me with Mr. Rosen at another point, as well. A notation toward the end of the transcript reads as follows:

"The witness was sworn in. He took an oath wearing a hat." (An alternate translation might be, "He took an oath with his head covered.")

This seems to be a reference to wearing a yarmulke or other religious head covering, but I never wear a yarmulke outside of synagogue, and I certainly wasn't wearing one at the trial. The identical notation is made at the end of Mr. Rosen's testimony, which, again, appears directly above my own in the transcript, so it seems logical that this physical detail was erroneously assigned to both of us.

A third and final correction:

On the second page of the transcript appears the following:

"I remember exactly the day when the night shift at the Schwarz Company was brought to the work camp and was killed. It was March 30, 1943."

The night shift was killed at the Piaski, not the work camp.

As I describe earlier in the book, workers were intercepted at the ghetto gates as they retuned home from a night of work, loaded into trucks, driven to the Piaski, and executed. The events of that morning are etched into my brain for all time; there is no mistaking them.

The next two sentences in this section read as follows:

"My sister was one of the people who worked at Schwarz and had to do the night shift on this day. I recognized my sister's clothes later at the place where the clothes were collected."

This detail does not appear earlier in the book . . . because I had forgotten. Or maybe I put it out of my mind. Seeing the words in the transcript brought it all back. "The place" referred to here is the Receiving Department at the DAW, where all the clothing of executed prisoners ended up (and where, later, I was assigned as a worker).

I remember sneaking into the area for several days after Clara's execution, rooting madly through piles of clothing until I found, as if by miracle, her dark cotton dress. It had a subtle pattern, I think. Plaid, or maybe floral. The sight of that crumpled, blood stained garment pulverized my heart into smithereens. No wonder the memory had escaped me with time. I am grateful to have it back.

Acknowledgments

The person who most inspired me to put my memories down in writing was Dr. Lisa Suzuki, Associate Professor at NYU's Steinhardt School of Culture, Education, and Human Development, who conducted a lengthy interview with me in April 2011, assisted by a fellow professor, my granddaughter Rachel Charatan, and family friends named Audrey and Sheldon Durst. In subsequent meetings and conversations, Dr. Suzuki impressed upon me how important it was to create a lasting record of my experiences, and encouraged me to find a collaborator who could help me write a memoir.

Elizabeth Edelstein, Director of Education at the Museum of Jewish Heritage — A Living Memorial to the Holocaust, has been a stalwart supporter of this undertaking. She introduced to me to Carl Capotorto, who, for several years, devoted himself tirelessly to the task of writing my story.

Dr. David Vorcheimer, formerly the Chief Cardiologist at Mount Sinai Hospital in New York, whose father had escaped Germany just under the wire in 1938, was also an important influence. Not only did he give me lifesaving medical care, which allowed me to pursue the writing of this book, but also took a keen interest in my stories about the Holocaust and encouraged me to tell them in written form.

Dr. Joel Shatzky, Professor Emeritus at SUNY Cortland, provided valuable help and assistance in the final stages of preparing the manuscript and accompanying photographs for publication.

Dr. Ilana Abramovich offered her time generously,

giving technical advice and assistance where it was needed.

Above all, I thank my family. My granddaughter, Rachel Charatan, has always been eager to hear about my experiences, and has long pressed me to record them for future generations. Her brother, my grandson Jimmy, invited me in 2004 to speak to a school group about the Holocaust, and has ever since encouraged me to immortalize the stories on paper. Joni Charatan, their mother, my daughter-in-law, has been an avid, helpful supporter and insightful reader.

Deborah Charatan, my niece, bemoaned the fact that her father never really talked about the war years before he died. Our entire clan had been murdered. Who were these people? When, where, and how had they been killed? Deborah asked me to make a written record so that the ancestors would not be lost to our family forever. Her brother, my nephew Eddie Charatan, felt the same way. Shirley Charatan Beck, their sister, my beloved niece, died of cancer on August 5, 2009, years before the book materialized, but I know she would have been proud and pleased. She was never far from my thoughts as I worked.

My sons Nat and Michael, and many other friends and family members, have also encouraged me over the years to leave a written account of my experiences for posterity. I am grateful to all.

 PHOTO ALBUM

From left to right: Dora and me with Vladek Neidziolka and his wife, Ann, when they traveled to America to attend our 50th anniversary party in 1999

Dora and Nat at Nat's Bar Mitzvah, 1963

Dora and me with our grandchildren, Jimmy and Rachel, in 1995

The guys and me at my second butcher shop, Lou's Meat Market, at 316 Franklin Avenue, Brooklyn, around 1951. From left to right: Nat, Teddy, Howie (holding pig tails), me, and Charlie (behind a bunch of sausages). My first shop, in another neighborhood, I gave to my father.

Ludwig Charatan

The gantze mishpucha at Eddie's Bar Mitzvah

My family and me in Krakow, 1946

Dora (right) as a young girl, around 1936, with a Christian friend of hers named Krzysia. The photo must have been folded for a while; the resulting fracture right down the middle, separating the girls, now seems prophetic.

Closed gates leading to a Piaski in Lvov, located just behind the Schrank house. This picture was taken in around 2010; the site is preserved as a kind of museum.

Clara (bottom left, with a sweater around her neck) with her public school classmates, years before the War began. She was around 12 years old at the time this picture was taken.

At Nat's Bar Mitzvah. Top row, left to right: My son Michael, me, Nat, Dora, Pepa, Jozek. Bottom row: Kasia, my father, my mother, my niece Shirley, my nephew Eddie. Seated in my father's lap is my niece Deborah.

Clockwise from top: Jozek, me, Dora, and Jozek's wife, Pepa, in New York City, 1970s

Left to right: Me, Dora and Jozek in Munich, around 1947

Staszko and a street performer in a bear suit, Krakow, 1945. Staszko came to visit . . . and my parents sent him home with 50,000 Polish zlotys.

Ludwig Charatan

Dora and me in America, 1950s

Ludwig Charatan

48463858R00100

Made in the USA
Lexington, KY
04 January 2016